What people are saying about

Jo Anne Allen's

MY SON IS A MARINE

"This Military Mom could start a new genre."
Bertrice Small, *NY Times* author

"Our young soldiers in Iraq appreciate heart-warming messages from home. Here's a meaningful gift for deployed troops."
Tara McPhail, wife of Capt. Charlie McPhail

"I know I couldn't have made it through deployment in Iraq and my recovery from injuries without my mom's support. I recommend this book to all military families."
Sgt. Sandra Perry, Medic

"And I thought two hanky reads had disappeared!"
Cindy Guyer, producer of Oxygen's
"Mr. Romance" reality series.

"Inspirational reading is needed for our recovering soldiers. I hope MY SON IS A MARINE will inspire more books of this type."

Chaplain Craig Wiley,
Walter Reed Army Medical Center

My Son is a Marine

Based on a true story

Jo Anne Allen

Echelon Press Publishing

Echelon Press
56 Sawyer Circle #354
Memphis, TN 38103

www.echelonpress.com

First Echelon Press paperback printing: July 2005
Copyright © 2005 by Jo Anne Allen and SOS America, Inc.

ISBN: 1-59080-447-3

10 9 8 7 6 5 4 3 2

Cover Art © Julie and Ken Barnes
ken.julie.barnes@verizon.net

Technical Design © Nathalie Moore

Printed in USA

I dedicate this to every military person serving our country. You deserve the highest honor and respect for your indomitable spirit in defending our country and keeping our nation free. May the Lord always have His special shield covering you to keep you safe and in His light.

Acknowledgments

I wish to thank my son, A.J., for inspiring me. It could only come from your precious heart. What a gift God gave me when you were born. As a writer, I cannot find the words to express my gratitude.

To Ken and Julie Barnes, you are true angels, for putting my son's letter into the right hands for publication and for designing this awesome book cover that depicts the story so perfectly.

To Kathryn Falk, founder SOS America, Inc., who made it possible for this story to become a book. You make a lot of people's dreams come true…and in this case, many more than you realize. God bless you!

Special thanks to my devoted friend, Suzanne Jaco-Raddle, for going above and beyond to educate me on computers and copy endless reams of my manuscripts for me, and for being such a powerful prayer partner throughout this process.

Great appreciation goes to my family and friends who have always believed in me and knew, without a doubt, that this book would become a reality.

I also wish to salute the members of SOS America, Inc. who have become wonderful friends and enriched my life.

To my dear friend and fellow author, Linda Fulkerson, thanks for taking the picture of me for the back cover.

Introduction

By Kathryn Falk, Lady of Barrow
Founder of Support Our Soldiers America, Inc.
CEO of RT BOOKclub Magazine

War makes strange bedfellows and creates a synchronicity we can only speculate upon.

In February of 2004, I launched Support Our Soldiers (SOS) America, Inc. to help our troops deployed overseas. Many were not receiving much mail and thought Americans were not behind them. They were also in need of vital supplies and homemade cookies.

Hundreds of RT BOOKclub readers joined me in writing letters, and shipping books, magazines, food, and toiletries to the front lines. None of us dreamed this involvement would lead to shepherding a book into publication. But spirituality joined with patriotism is a powerful force. Many members were establishing a close bond with particular Marines and soldiers. Letters and emails flew back and forth. When graphics artist Julie Barnes forwarded a heart-wrenching letter from one of her pen pals, it was included in our SOS newsletter.

So far from home, and under great stress, the young Marine was desperately worried about his ailing father who was looked after full-time by his mother. He asked if we could help his mother in Arkansas get published. "She's a pretty good story teller," he added. "If she could get published, maybe the family won't lose our family farm."

SOS members mobilized. I called Mrs. Allen. Like most military moms, she stayed close to the phone, hoping to hear from her son occasionally. She had writing experience but had never targeted a mainstream market. After talking with her, I felt compelled to suggest that she write what she was going through with a son in the war. Although memoirs of the Iraqi conflict existed, I'd not seen one from a mother's point of view. She said she would pray for divine inspiration.

Ten days later, I received the first draft of MY SON IS A MARINE. I was so moved by the story that I stayed up all night to finish it. I called and congratulated her, and said we would support her.

Of course, the accompanying box of homemade peanut butter cookies were melt-in-your mouth delicious. It was almost enough for me to run out and follow her recipe. I gave a sample to friends who agreed they were *fabuloso*.

Fortunately, SOS America includes some of the top experts in the book industry. I was able to enlist book doctor, Mary K., to edit and polish the prose. Julie and Ken Barnes agreed to design the cover. And, when I sent the finished manuscript to Karen Syed of Echelon Press, she loved it and agreed to be the publisher. Buyers and distributors agreed to help with moving copies into bookstores and military bases.

I thank all of our SOS America members for contributing to this project in one way or another. Part of the proceeds of MY SON IS A MARINE will help our efforts to support our troops, particularly the injured at Walter Reed Hospital.

Semper Fi,
Kathryn Falk, Lady of Barrow
Brooklyn, New York
Email: barrowlady@aol.com

A note to the reader...

Before sitting down with this book, it is highly recommended that you bake a batch of the incredible peanut butter cookies (recipe is located on page 191) and enjoy them as you savor every word.

෴   ෴

"I can't believe it's not butter in those *fabuloso* peanut butter cookies."

–Fabio

My Son is a Marine

PROLOGUE

"Hello?" I asked hesitantly as I picked up the ringing telephone.

"Mom?"

My heart dropped. This was the phone call I had expected, yet dreaded, from my eighteen-year-old son, A.J.

"Hi, A.J."

"I told you I'd call to say good-bye. We leave for Kuwait in twenty minutes," he said matter-of-factly.

My eyes welled up with tears, but I swallowed the big lump in my throat and asked, "What do you want in your first care package?"

"Can you make me those peanut butter cookies I like so much?" he asked.

"You bet," I said enthusiastically, as if he were heading off to college.

"I was told I'll be over there a whole year. Write often…okay, Mom?"

"Of course, I will. And I'll be praying very hard. I love you, A.J."

"Thanks, Mom. I love you, too. I have to go now."

I hung up the phone and sat quietly at the kitchen table.

It was really happening–it wasn't just rumors anymore. The country was about to go to war. And my son would be on the front lines.

A.J. was just a boy. *My* boy. What if I never saw

him again?

"Do you know how much I love you, A.J.? Do you have any Earthly idea what you mean to me?" I said aloud, as tears streamed down my face.

Then, knowing it would be all too easy to let myself become hysterical, I grabbed my head with both hands, closed my eyes, clenched my teeth together, and prayed for the strength to make the negative thoughts go away.

What God gave me instead was a barrage of memories.

Eighteen years go by fast. Had I thought I could protect A.J. his whole life? Like a mother hen who shields her chicks from danger by having them hide under her, I wanted to whisk my son out of harm's way.

But a mother hen knows an unprotected chick is vulnerable and easily snared. A.J. was neither. He was a United States Marine. He had completed thirteen weeks of grueling boot camp. How many people could say they'd made it through that hell?

Now he was headed to Kuwait. He was part of an elite group of young men and women who were going to fight terrorism. War hadn't been officially declared yet, but everyone knew that preparations had been made. It was only a matter of time....

I was scared. War is a terrifying word. And so I did the only thing I *could* do to protect both my sanity and my son. I prayed.

"Oh, God, please...I know you've heard these same prayers over and over from thousands of mothers just like me. But it's unnatural for parents to outlive their children. You tell us that we're given only what we can handle. I couldn't handle losing A.J. Look at my life, Lord. I've tried to be strong through all the other heartaches. Please, take care of Your child and mine. Please...*please*...take care of all of them."

My Son is a Marine

ONE

My name is Jo Anne Allen. I am the mother of a Marine stationed in Iraq.

We all have a story. I would like to tell you mine. I want to share with you how very special my son is. Most people never know how much of an impact their existence makes on others. With A.J., though, it's clear that there would be a big hole in the universe if he had never been born. Maternal bias and pride aside, I can tell you, he's done a lot in his short years upon the Earth.

So let's start at the beginning.

We lived in Denver, Colorado. It was May third, 1984. Since I was three weeks past due with my second child, my husband and I decided to let my obstetrician induce labor. It was a very difficult delivery. Unlike his older bother Bo, this little boy came out screaming and yelling. We named him Aaron Jacob, but we soon started calling him A.J. With his gorgeous brown eyes and dark hair, I thought he was simply beautiful.

At the age of three, A.J. was always busy creating chaos in the family. His two brothers–Bo, three years older, and Darin, two years younger–were on the quiet side and enjoyed the swing set, kiddie swimming pools, and cartoons. A.J. dangled from the monkey bars, splashed all the water out of the kiddie pool, and stood in front of the television, bouncing on his feet, to watch Inspector Gadget. If my backyard was quiet, I knew A.J. wasn't outside. If my house was quiet, I knew A.J. wasn't inside.

He was my social butterfly. He loved saying hello to everyone in the neighborhood. At his tender age, he befriended two young girls who lived across the street. Many times, with supervision, he rode his little bike–his favorite toy, with its mini-training wheels–to their house to play. The girls' father often sat outside and supervised them.

One particular day, A.J. was playing with the girls. My husband, Randy, and I had company, and I had prepared a steak and shrimp dinner. Everything was ready, and I went to the front door to ask my neighbor to send A.J. home to eat.

I went back to the kitchen and within seconds heard a sickening sound that made my stomach turn over, then instantly tie itself in knots: screeching tires followed by ear-piercing screams. No one had to tell me what had happened. I knew A.J. had been hit by a car.

I ran to the front door but didn't see A.J. anywhere. His small crumpled bike was tangled under the front bumper of a car stopped in the middle of the street. My heart pounded as hard as it ever had as my gaze scanned the street in front of the vehicle.

There he was–lying in the middle of the road, folded up like an accordion.

I raced toward him, oblivious of the gathering crowd. Vaguely, I heard someone say they'd called 911 and that the MedEvac helicopter was on its way. But I had no attention for anything but A.J. Instinct took over as I fell to my knees beside him. The few seconds it took me to determine that he was unconscious, but not dead were, without a doubt, the worst moments of my life.

I realize now how foolish it was to ignore the helpful advice of my neighbors not to move, or even touch, him. Looking back, I guess I thought he needed to be out of the street. So I gently slid my hands under his tiny frame, lifted him in my arms, and took him to my driveway, where I lay him down and hovered over him.

At that point, I became aware that Randy was speaking angrily to a bunch of teenagers–the ones who'd been in the car. The driver, who couldn't have been more than sixteen, was muttering that he hadn't seen A.J. crossing the road on his bike. Our neighbor, who'd been watching, was yelling back at the boy, saying that he'd seen the car come screeching around the corner and tear down the street as if it were a NASCAR speedway–and it was just "damned lucky" the car wasn't very powerful and that there hadn't been time after turning the corner to pick up much speed.

The argument ended when Flight for Life–the MedEvac team from Aurora–arrived, at the same time a police car rolled to a stop and the officers in it herded the teenagers and our neighbor off to talk to them.

Randy and I watched, arms around each other, as the paramedics examined A.J. and prepared him for transport. As they worked, they tossed around terms I didn't understand and said things that served to heighten my nearly out-of-control anxiety: internal bleeding...broken femur that could have severed the femoral artery when he'd been moved...concussion and swelling as a result of an obvious blow to the head. I'd noticed the bump on A.J.'s head when I'd–wrongly–moved him, but by this time, his head had swelled to twice its normal size.

The paramedics strapped A.J. to a backboard and

whisked him away. We left our dinner guests in charge of our other two children and drove frantically to the hospital where A.J. had been taken.

When we arrived at the emergency room, we asked for A.J., and the nurse pointed to the surgical area and told us that the ER doctors were examining him.

Again, at that point, maternal instinct took over, and I did something I would never have done under normal circumstances. I simply had to know my son's condition, so I burst into the trauma room, uninvited. What I saw nearly made me faint–the heart monitor displaying a single unbroken line. I knew what that meant. A.J.'s heart had stopped.

I slapped both hands over my mouth, but that did little to muffle my scream. "No! Oh, God! A.J., no!"

"Get her out of here!" one of the doctors said abruptly.

The last thing I remember as a nurse ushered me out of the trauma room were the faces of several people working furiously to get A.J.'s heart re-started.

Randy and I were taken to a private waiting room with only a clock on the wall, several chairs, and a coffee table strewn with old magazines.

We sat down, and a minute later, he admitted to me he was worried that A.J. would have brain damage, that, after all, he'd been thrown twenty feet and landed on his head. I was worried A.J. was dead. I couldn't begin to process what it would mean if he weren't dead but that he would have to face life as a vegetable.

Randy and I held hands and prayed together. I tried my best to have faith, to feel optimistic, but sitting there in that impersonal, dingy room, I couldn't help but fear the worst.

A little over an hour passed before the doctor came. Randy and I stood and clutched each other's hand, waiting for him to tell us the news–waiting to hear whether or not our son was alive.

The doctor–a short, dark-haired man of about forty– gave us a brief, tired smile. "Your son has a concussion."

Has. Present tense. My heart started beating again.

"He had a very serious blow to his head," the doctor continued. "We did an MRI and ultrasound and, amazingly, found nothing but swelling. His brain is normal."

At that, I couldn't entirely stifle the sob that escaped me. Randy's grip tightened on my hand.

Then the doctor shook his head. "His heart did stop once, but we were able to resuscitate him. He's been in and out of consciousness, but his vital signs are stable."

At that, I began crying so hard I barely heard the rest of what the doctor had to say.

"He's on his way into surgery right now. He has a ruptured spleen that's causing a lot of internal bleeding, and it has to be removed. And his broken femur will also be set."

A broken leg seemed inconsequential. Bones mended. But...spleens–what did I know about them? Not much. Something vague about football players losing theirs a lot and being perfectly fine afterward.

"Also," the doctor continued, "you need to know that part of A.J.'s optical nerve was severed. We think it will repair itself in time, but he might need glasses when he gets older."

Beside me, I felt more than heard Randy heave in a

great gulp of air and let it out. "Thank you, doctor. When can we see him?"

"When he comes out of recovery and we take him to his room, I'll have someone show you where it is." He gave an encouraging smile. "I'd say you both are mighty lucky parents. This could have been so much worse."

If the doctor said anything after that, I didn't hear it. I was crying again and thanking God, and all I could think about was seeing A.J.

It was several hours before we were taken to A.J.'s room. We found him asleep. Although bruised and swollen, his sedated body looked peaceful.

We decided that I would spend the night with A.J. while Randy went home. I sat in the chair all night, watching my son sleep, thinking about all the joy he had brought us...and praying.

Around 7:00 a.m., while the nursing shifts were changing, I went to the cafeteria for coffee. When I returned, I found A.J.'s room in a state of chaos. For an instant, as I approached, my anxiety level increased, but then I saw the smiling expressions on the medical personnel who were rushing in and out of the room. They asked me, please, to wait in the hall, saying that everything was all right–but that A.J. was sharing his wonderful experience with them, and the doctor wanted to hear it in its entirety, without interruption.

I had no idea what they were talking about, but knowing A.J., I thought I could imagine. My always enthusiastic son was entertaining the doctor. I wondered which of his childhood experiences he was relating in his inimitable excited and dramatic tones.

After waiting outside for what seemed like forever, I

was finally allowed to enter the room. A.J. was sitting up in bed, broken leg elevated, and grinning from ear to ear.

"Mama!" he exclaimed with a note of joy I'd never heard before. "I saw God!"

I looked at the others in the room–a female nurse and three young male interns. They were all smiling at me.

One of the interns must have realized–probably because of my baffled expression–that I was waiting for an explanation. "Your son had an out-of-body experience," he announced as he stood next to A.J. "Apparently, it happens sometimes to people who've clinically died, then been resuscitated. Your son's chart says his heart stopped yesterday, and it took several tries with the defibrillator to get him back. In a technical sense, he was dead for over two minutes. So it seems that during those two minutes, A.J. got a little glimpse of Heaven."

By this time, my eyebrows were stretched upward as far as they would go.

Reading my skepticism correctly, the nurse took over the conversation. "A.J. has told each of us exactly the same story. He's not imagining things or fibbing. We're trained to know when someone is fabricating a story, and I'm as certain as I can be that A.J. is telling the truth."

"Yeah, Mama!" A.J. chimed in. "And Grandma isn't dead like you think. She's just fine! I saw her first."

I believed him. Even without the nurse's testimony, I didn't have a bit of doubt that, somehow, A.J. had seen my mother.

I wanted to be alone with him. I had a million questions. *Tell me about Grandma! What does God look like? Did you see other people, too? What did the angels look like? Were they really huge? Did they have wings? Tell me everything!*

After the hospital staff left the room, I tried to keep the tears welling in my eyes from spilling over, but it was impossible. I sat down next to A.J. on the bed and held his small little hands in mine.

"Don't cry, Mama," he said.

I swiped at the tears on my cheeks, then brought his forehead to rest against mine. "Thank you, God," I whispered.

"Mama! I have to tell you about God!"

I smiled, but the tears came even harder. What had that intern said? *"Your son had an out- of-body experience."* How many three-year-olds could say that? For that matter, how many people could say that? Very few, I guessed.

"That's incredible, sweetheart," I said. "Tell me all about it."

"Well," he began as the light sparkled in his eyes. "First I saw you crying when you were holding me on our driveway. Then, the helicopter came, and they put me inside. Grandma was with me the whole time. Then I got to a big room, and that's when I found out I could fly. Me and Grandma were way up in the clouds!"

I paid close attention, as I knew A.J. had been unconscious and could not possibly have known about my holding him or the trip to the hospital in the helicopter.

"Then–" he nearly bounced on the bed with excitement– "I saw lots of other angels, all flying around me. I wanted to hold their hands, but they wouldn't let me, not even Grandma. They said the rule was I would have to stay if I touched them. So I didn't."

I shook my head. "Really?"

"Nope. I didn't touch them. And I wanted to 'cause they were *soooo* pretty! They had giant feathers on their wings, and they smiled at me, and we were all floating in the clouds! And then they said I could wish for anything I wanted to eat and pull a piece of the cloud off, and when I put it in my mouth, it would taste like my favorite thing!"

A.J.'s excitement was contagious. I was smiling and crying and watching his face as he told me the story. It was almost too much for me to take. I wanted to let each word sink in slowly. I still couldn't get over the fact that he was just fine. No brain damage whatsoever. How blessed I felt then, to have been given this precious little boy–twice, it seemed.

"Can I guess what you wished the cloud tasted like?" I asked, trying to involve myself in his unbelievable experience.

"You know," he said, grinning.

"Tell me anyway."

"Peanut butter cookies!" he said. "And I did pull off a piece of cloud, Mama! I did what they told me to do. I stuck it in my mouth, and it tasted just like your peanut butter cookies!"

"Wow," I said. What else was there to say?

"Wait till I tell you the best part! After that, they said God wanted to see me. So they took me to God, and He said–"

"Whoa!" I held up my hand. "A.J., slow down. Tell me this part real slowly. How did they take you to God? Where was God? God wanted to see you?"

"Mama! *I'm* telling you the story. All the angels and Grandma were there. Then I was alone with God. He wears the whitest clothes you ever saw, and He has real long white hair, and He doesn't laugh, but He smiles a lot. He folded His arms like this." A.J. crossed his little arms across his chest. "He said 'A.J., you go home.' So I came home."

I waited for more. So much more. I wanted him to tell me the story over and over again. It was so incredible. My mother had passed away the year before from cancer. She and A.J. had been very close, and when she died, he hadn't truly understood what death meant. What two-year-old would?

It seemed, however, that his experience had given him an understanding far beyond his years.

"Is that all God told you?" I prompted.

A.J. was hesitant. "He...well, He said another thing, Mama. He said I had to come back because I needed to do something real important for Him when I get older."

"What?" I asked, both curious and a little wary.

A.J. shrugged his small shoulders. "I don't know. He just said it would be something real important."

"What do you think it is? He didn't give you any idea?"

A.J. shrugged again. "Nope. I think...I think He's keeping it a secret."

I stared at my son, my heart beating fast. A secret? What kind of secret purpose did God have in mind for my son?

I wasn't sure I wanted to know.

During the months his leg was in a cast, A.J. couldn't romp and play as he normally did. His brothers kept him company some of the time. But Bo had his own, older friends, and Darin, at two, was still too much a baby to keep A.J. occupied for long.

Most often it fell to me to help A.J. pass the time. I told him stories and read to him from books that I remembered fondly from my own childhood. A.J. loved those stories and asked to hear them over and over. Although it was tedious for me to repeat them for the twentieth time, I did it–anything to keep him from becoming bored and depressed in his forced confinement.

"The three trees, Mama! Tell me the story about the three trees again!"

I rolled my eyes and relaxed my shoulders in exasperation. "A.J., you've heard that story so many times! How about if I read *The Big Hungry Bear* instead? Then we can look at the pictures."

"No! I like the Three Trees. It's my favorite. *Please....*"

"Your dad tells it better than I do," I tried to negotiate.

"I like your way," A.J. insisted.

His brown eyes melted my heart. They always did. And so I began....

"Once upon a time there were three trees on a hill, in the woods," I said.

"You forgot to say 'long, long ago,'" A.J. reminded me.

I closed my eyes and sighed. My son did not miss a trick.

"Once upon a time, *long, long ago*...there were three trees on a hill, in the woods."

A.J. giggled with delight and put his head on my chest.

I smiled. "These three trees were all discussing their number-one dreams and hopes for the future. The first tree said, 'Someday I want to be a treasure chest. I want to be filled with gold and silver and all the precious jewels of the Earth. I want to have intricate carvings and beautiful decorations for all the world to see.' Then the second tree said, "My wish is to...""

"No!" A.J. interrupted. "You need to have a different voice to be the other tree."

"Sorry, I forgot," I whispered, then continued. "The second tree said, 'My wish is to be a mighty ship. I could take kings and queens across the seas and sail across all the waters to the farthest corners of the world. I will be a very powerful and strong ship, and all who ride on me will be safe.'

"Now, the third tree was different. He was happy being a tree. He said," my voice dropped to its lowest register, "'I just want to be a tree–a tall, straight tree. And all who look up to see me on top of this hill will be looking toward Heaven, and it will make them think of God.'"

I paused to glance at A.J.'s face. He seemed so peaceful, so serene. I wondered if the reason he wanted to hear this story so often was because it reminded him of how close he'd once been to God.

Returning to the story, I said, "Over the next few years, the trees spent all their time praying that their dreams would come true. Then one day, a group of woodsmen came out of the forest at the foot of the hill, saw the three trees at the top, and climbed the hill to look at them. One man went up to the first tree and said, 'Hey! I think I'll cut this tree down and sell it to a carpenter.'

"That made the first tree very happy, because it just knew its fondest wish was about to be granted. The carpenter would turn it into a treasure chest.

"The second woodsman looked at the second tree and said," I pitched my voice higher, "'Just look at this tree! It's so tall and straight, it would make a perfect mast for a sailing ship. I'll cut it down and sell it to a shipyard.' And so he began chopping, which made the second tree very happy, because he, too, knew that his prayers had been answered. He would become part of a mighty ship, sailing before the wind."

A.J. was playing with his toes that stuck out of his cast, but I knew he was totally engrossed in the story.

"The last woodsman approached the third tree, making the tree quake with fright. Remember, it wanted to grow tall and straight, high on the hill, so that people who looked up at it would think of God. If the woodsman cut it down, its dream would be lost forever. And that's exactly what happened. The woodsman said, 'I don't need this tree for anything special, but I'll cut it down anyway.' And he chopped with his axe until the great tree fell, then hauled it away, taking the tree's dream with him."

When I paused, A.J.'s head came up, and his gaze shot toward me. "But that's not the end!" he exclaimed.

"I know." I chuckled as I rubbed the natural curls on his head. Then, after he'd settled back against me again, I went on.

"As it turned out, the first tree was sold to the carpenter and made into a feed box for animals. He was put into a barn and filled with hay, which made him very sad because that wasn't what he had prayed for at all.

"The second tree was sad, too, when he was cut up

and made into a small fishing boat. He had wanted to carry kings and queens across the high seas, but the only person who ever used him was a lowly fisherman, and he never got out of sight of the shore.

"The third tree was cut into large pieces and stacked in a dark place that never saw the light of the sun. And so the years went slowly by, and the three trees forgot all about their dreams."

I paused for effect, and, right on cue, A.J. drew a quick breath and blurted out, "Don't stop! Something else happens then."

I had to laugh. "Yes, something happens. One day, a man and woman came into the barn where the first tree had been placed as a feed box for animals. The woman gave birth to a baby boy. Her husband wanted to make a crib for the baby, but they were traveling, and he had no tools or wood with him. So he filled the manger with clean hay and placed the baby in it. It would have to do.

"Somehow, the first tree felt the importance of the moment. It knew the baby lying in it was special–and it knew its dream had come true. It was holding the greatest treasure of all time!"

"The baby Jesus," A.J. exclaimed.

"Yes, it was holding baby Jesus," I said. "Then, some years later, a group of men got into the small fishing boat made from the second tree. One of these men was tired and went to sleep. While they were out on the water, a great storm came and rocked the boat back and forth, back and forth. It rocked it so hard that the boat didn't think it was strong enough to keep the men safe. The frightened men woke up the sleeping man.

"The sleeping man stood inside the boat and said, 'Be

still!' And all at once, the storm stopped, as if it had never happened.

"At that moment, the second tree felt its ultimate wish had come true. It knew it was carrying the King of Kings in the boat it had become.

"It was carrying Jesus!" A.J. declared.

"Yes," I agreed. "Now, soon afterward, a group of men went into the dark place where the third tree lay cut up in large pieces, and they took one long chunk from the stack. The tree was given to one man to carry, and as he lugged its heavy weight through the streets, it listened as people mocked the man.

"The man dragged the tree all the way up to the top of the hill where it had grown. There, on that Friday morning, the man was nailed to the tree, which was then raised and staked so it stood pointing toward Heaven. And the other people left the man there until he died. Then they cut him down and carried him away, leaving the tree standing at the top of the hill. The tree was very, very sad about what it had witnessed and the part it had played. It wondered how God could have let it be used for such a wicked purpose.

"It rained all the rest of that day, and the next. Then, on Sunday morning, the sun rose brighter than the tree had ever seen it. And, suddenly, somehow, it realized that its ultimate dream had come true. It knew that all the people who'd stood watching the man die had been thinking about God. And it knew that, for that short time, it had been closer to God than anyone had ever been before."

Knowing A.J. loved to finish the story himself, I smiled down at him. "Why was that, do you think?"

"Because Jesus was crucified on it," he said.

"And were the three trees all happy?"

"Yes! They were very happy!"

"But why did they ever doubt that their wishes would come true?"

"Because," A.J. said, grinning, "God has lots of secrets. *He* knew they'd all get what they wanted. He just gave it to them in different ways than they thought they'd get it. We think God should do things *our* way, but He almost never does. He has His own way. And it's always better."

Hearing the certain knowledge in A.J.'s childish voice, I was struck—as I had been many times since his accident—by his utter conviction. His faith. Guiltily, I wished my own faith, strong as it was, were as unwavering as my young son's.

But then, I hadn't met God. And I hadn't a single doubt that A.J.'s wisdom and understanding—his spiritual maturity—was the direct result of his near-death experience. It stunned me slightly to realize that I was changing, too, because of A.J.'s experience. His faith was strengthening mine. God had given A.J. a tiny glimpse of Heaven, then had sent him back to teach me what it meant truly to believe.

In the dark days that lay far ahead in our future, unforeseen and completely unplanned for, I looked back many times on that sunny morning and was grateful for God's gift of my son.

TWO

We were living in years of plenty. Both Randy and I had great jobs and, together, were bringing in a six-figure income. Consequently, my children's memory banks are crammed with trips to Lake Powell, Las Vegas, Keystone for skiing, Yellowstone National Park, Disneyland, and even a cruise to the Bahamas.

We had an Olympic-size trampoline, a huge speedboat, and a loaded camping trailer. Every weekend was spent on the lake or in the mountains. A.J. and his brothers became good at snow skiing, snow boarding, all water sports, and fishing. We did manage to make it to church most Sundays before heading out on another family adventure. Life was good, and we felt very blessed.

A.J. loved dogs, so we got him a white Jack Russell terrier for his thirteenth birthday. He named her Marcie, taught her lots of tricks, and spoiled her relentlessly. The two of them were inseparable.

Although Marcie slept with A.J., he still insisted on stories every night. He liked to hear me reminisce about things he had done in his younger days that had amused, angered, baffled, or shocked me–sometimes, all at once. He also loved "God stories," as he called them, especially if they included Jesus. His favorite, however, was the well-known modern poem "Footprints in the Sand," only recently attributed to Mary Stevenson, who is believed to have written it in 1936.

Around this same time, Randy and I decided to invest in a farm in Arkansas. My mother grew up on Mount Magazine, so I had personal knowledge of the great summers, mild winters, and laid-back attitudes of the locals. I wanted that after living in the fast lane for so long. We decided we'd use our farm for vacations for a few more years, pay it off, and then move there when we retired. We had a plan!

Our first summer in Arkansas was great. A.J. brought a friend with him, and they were mesmerized by the lightning bugs, huge chicken snakes, toads, lizards, and everything that 'creepeth' upon the Earth. We even had a pond on our fifty-plus acres, which meant the boys spent a lot of time fishing.

Over the course of the summer, we moved our "toys" to the farm. The boat and the camper were first. Then we added two four-wheelers, a riding lawn mower, and a jet ski. We were amazed to discover that there was never a wait to get on the lake with it.

A.J. was fourteen years old when Randy and I decided to make Arkansas our year-round home. We quit our jobs, packed up everything, and became residents.

At first, devastated by culture shock, the boys had a hard time adjusting to rural life. The schools were stricter, and even the language the locals spoke seemed different, with it's Southern accent and idioms. Not long after we'd moved, the boys all informed us that, at age eighteen, they were moving back to colorful Colorado. Slowly, though, they adjusted—in varying degrees.

A.J.'s adjustment was made easier by his outgoing personality. He made friends quickly, one of whom was a neighbor boy named Billy. The two of them liked to ride between our place and Billy's on one of our four-wheelers. As Arkansas law allows fourteen-year-olds to drive farm equipment, and as they mostly stayed on the dirt roads on our and Billy's land, crossing only one two-lane highway to get between farms, I saw no harm in it.

Well, all parents make mistakes. I just thank God each day that the ones I've made haven't yet proved fatal–although some have come too close for comfort.

One day, A.J. and Billy crossed the road between farms in the four-wheeler without noticing a truck barreling toward them. The truck struck the four-wheeler, then went into a spin.

I was called to the scene immediately, and the first thing I saw was the four-wheeler lying in a crumpled heap under the truck, which was obviously totaled.

Like that awful day when A.J. was hit while riding his little bike across our street, my heart pounded like a jack hammer as my gaze searched the road in front the wrecked vehicles. But neither A.J. nor Billy was anywhere in sight.

By this time, I was shivering from head to toe with fear, and it only got worse when one of the policeman who arrived on the scene told me they thought the boys were trapped under the truck with the demolished four-wheeler. Bo and Darin were with me, and the officer tried to prepare us for the worst.

The idea that A.J. was lying squashed under that truck was devastating, unthinkable. Billy's mother held on to me, using my smaller frame to support hers.

It seemed to take forever for the fire department and wrecking crew to separate the two vehicles. When they did, it came as a shock to everyone to discover that A.J.

and Billy weren't there. They simply were gone. Witnesses, including the driver of the truck, who had escaped unharmed, had already said they saw both boys on the four-wheeler as the truck hit it.

But there was no blood on either vehicle or on the road. And no mangled bodies.

As we were all standing there, totally bewildered–and, in my case, as close to hysterical as I've ever been–something very strange happened.

"Mom, look!" Bo said, pointing across the road, into a large, half-grown field of corn.

There, in the distance, walking toward us, were the two boys. As they drew closer, I could see A.J.'s expression–confused and disoriented.

"We woke up in the field," were his first words as he and Billy came to a stop in front of us.

My gaze shot back and forth from him to his friend, who looked equally confused. "What are you talking about? Where have you been?" I asked, hearing the strain, as well as the disbelief, in my own voice.

A.J. looked around at the police, Billy's mother, the neighbors, the nervous male driver of the truck, then back to me. "Mom, we were on the four-wheeler–and then we weren't. Somehow, we were asleep in that field. We both woke up a few minutes ago, and neither of us know what happened. I can't explain it better than that."

I shook my head and gestured toward the truck's driver. "A.J., this man ran into you! He said you didn't even look when you crossed the road."

A.J. glanced at Billy, who still appeared bewildered. He then checked himself over–front and back, up and down–before letting his gaze move slowly over everyone gathered at the scene. The policemen, our neighbors, the truck driver, Bo and Darin, and me: All of us were waiting for a rational explanation.

Clearly, A.J. interpreted correctly the doubt on our faces, for when he spoke again, his tone was almost angry. "Then you tell me what happened, Mom," he said. "If we got hit by a truck, where's the blood? Why aren't we hurt? I tell you, I am not lying!" Pointing behind him, he shouted, "We were *asleep in that field*."

It was obvious that no one believed a word of what he'd said. Yet no one, not even the police, could argue with his reasoning. In the end, the police just wrote down A.J.'s "explanation," the wrecking crew hauled away the vehicles, and everyone went home, grateful that no one had been hurt but unsatisfied.

I couldn't stop thinking about A.J.'s accident. It wasn't logical. I questioned him several times, and he always seemed evasive. Finally, I couldn't stand it any longer. I wanted–needed–more information.

The door to his room was slightly ajar, and I knocked before pushing it wider and entering. "A.J.?"

"I know, I know," he said, "I'm getting into bed now."

"I was going to ask if you wanted to hear a story."

His brown eyes sparkled. "Always!" He plopped onto the bed and scooted his feet under the covers.

I sat on the edge of the mattress, moved Marcie over to make room, and began. "Did I ever tell you about the time you first announced that you wanted a pet?"

A.J. gave me that irresistible toothy grin of his. "You mean the goldfish?"

I nodded.

"Go for it, parental unit," he said grabbing Marcie in his arms, then settling back on the pillows.

"Well...we decided to start you out with two goldfish, figuring that if you took care of them, we could advance to something with fur. So you and I went to the pet store and picked out two pretty, orange, buggy-eyed goldfish. I got the little rocks, the bowl, the silly fake castle, and the food for them, and I showed you how to take care of them."

Frowning thoughtfully, A.J. asked, "Weren't they the same fish that Darin wanted to feed? He was still really little...like three, maybe. He stuck an entire hot dog in the bowl and said they could eat on that for a long time."

"Yes," I agreed, chuckling. "He thought he was helping. Anyway, a few days passed, and...well, if I didn't hear you in the house, I used to come looking for you because I knew you were up to something. Do you remember what happened?"

"I just wanted to hold them!" he exclaimed. "I remember they were so slippery, and then they kept wiggling, and I couldn't keep them in my hand!"

I laughed. "You squeezed the poor things to death! When I came into your room, you had something really gross in your hand, and you put your hand behind your back to hide it from me. But I insisted on seeing what it was."

"You thought I was picking my nose," he added. "You lectured me about using Kleenex, and you made me wash my hands."

"Yes," I agreed. "Then I just happened to look at the goldfish bowl–and there were two orange *things* floating at the top! A.J., they had no eyes!"

He couldn't stop laughing. "I was just a little kid, Mom! I didn't know better. You ought to know I felt terrible about it. I really prayed God would forgive me because I didn't *mean* to kill them. I just wanted to hold them!"

Now was my cue. "Okay. I told you a story. Now, you tell me one."

A.J. looked surprised, but he just shrugged and said, "Sure. What do you want to hear?"

I hesitated only a second. "What really happened when you wrecked the four- wheeler?"

His expression went from relaxed to solemn in a flash. "Don't you buy the story I already told you?" he asked warily.

"No."

"Everyone else does."

"A.J., I'm your mother. I know you better than anyone else, and I know there's something more to it than what you told the police. Please, tell me what happened."

He took a deep breath, closed his eyes for a second or two, then opened them again and looked at me. "I'll only tell you if you promise that we won't ever talk about it again–and that you won't tell anybody else, not even Dad."

I chewed my bottom lip, debating if I could keep such a promise. Finally, I said, "All right. I promise, I'll keep it between us."

He took another deep breath. Then, in a rush, he said, "Mom, the Lord saved us. We were taken to that field by angels. Billy claims he doesn't remember, and maybe he doesn't. It was like we'd been knocked out, so he probably thinks he dreamed it. But I know it was real–

because the Lord gave me a message. He told me I was to be more careful. He reminded me that it was the second time He'd saved my life and...and that..."

"And...what?" I asked softly, hearing my voice quaver.

"And that He had a job for me. He said He needed me for something in the future, and that it was really important to Him and that I was to watch out for myself better." His eyebrows drawn together in a deep frown, A.J. shot me a quick glance. "That's it. Now, are you satisfied?"

Satisfied? Hardly. I didn't know *what* I felt, except that satisfied wasn't it.

Oh, I believed what A.J. had told me. I knew he wasn't lying. But what was this "something" for which God needed my son so badly that He would save A.J.'s life–not once but twice, now? The possibilities flashed through my mind like clips from an old-fashioned newsreel. From the glorious to the terrifying, none of them did anything to ease my mind.

Life turns on a dime. We all know that. None of us are guaranteed that our skies will always be blue or that life will always be easy. Things happen in a second that change our lives forever.

A.J.'s life was changed in the summer of 2000, when his friend Billy was hit and killed by a drunk driver. A.J. went very quiet for several months afterward, his natural exuberance tempered by grief. My heart ached for him, but all I could do was remind him that he could be sure that Billy was with God. After all, he himself had seen what awaited us after death. That seemed to help.

Then, on January 13, 2001, at 11:30 a.m., life changed for all the Allens.

Randy had been working outside, in the rain, all morning. He came into the back room, with his muddy boots, and fell over. I heard him collapse and ran to see what had happened.

He looked bewildered as he tried to get up. I questioned him, and he said he'd tripped. I thought he must have broken his hip or leg. He was acting strangely, but I couldn't put my finger on it.

By then, Bo was in college, in Denver, so I called for Darin and A.J. to come help.

Together, the boys lifted their father into a chair. That's when we noticed that his entire left side was limp. Completely limp. Plus, he was slurring his words and sweating profusely. I knew these were all signs of a stroke, but I couldn't believe it. It was unreal. Impossible. My forty-six-year-old husband was a healthy man. Healthy men his age didn't have strokes out of the blue like this. Did they?

A.J. and Darin were horrified. We called an ambulance immediately. Then, when the paramedics had left with Randy, we got ourselves together quickly and went to the hospital in Little Rock.

A doctor met us at the ER. He said that Randy was in critical condition. Either he would pull out of this in seventy-two hours, or his brain would continue to swell— and he would die.

Vaguely, through my own haze of shocked terror, I was aware that A.J. and Darin were equally afraid.

"What happened?" I demanded. "He *can't* have had a stroke! He's never even been sick!"

The doctor was very kind but firm. "Your husband's right carotid artery was completely blocked, and it cut off the blood flow to his brain," he explained. "I'm sorry, Mrs. Allen. It's quite rare to see a man so young have this happen to him. Usually these things occur much later in life." Pausing briefly, glancing at A.J. and Darin, he added, "Now would be a good time to notify the rest of your family members. Your husband is in critical condition, and the prognosis isn't good."

The words *not expected to live* flashed through my mind. He hadn't said it, but that's what he meant.

A.J., Darin, and I called the rest of the family. Linda, my dear friend from Denver, brought Bo home, and she stood by my side throughout those awful seventy-two hours. Randy's mother, sisters, brothers, and niece were also there. It was a dark time.

Prayer is powerful. We sent word out to everyone we could think of, and throughout the grim hours, we could feel the prayers working.

Randy survived those crucial seventy-two hours. Still, the stroke had done a lot of damage. The doctors talked about physical therapy, but we could tell from their tone that it would be years, if ever, before Randy could re-gain some of what was lost. Whether he did or not, we were in for a lot of heartache.

Since he was totally confined to a wheelchair, I was forced to stay home and take care of him, which meant quitting my job. I had a healthy 401k and planned to use *some* of the money to live on until I figured things out.

A.J. was a junior, and Darin was in the eighth grade. Neither of them could be expected to contribute to the family income for some time; on the contrary, I had college for both of them to think about. I was also determined that Bo be able to finish his degree.

It wasn't long before the "toys" were sold. We decided as a family that it wouldn't be fair to leave Randy home while we had fun. We would wait until he was able to join us again. We all just knew, regardless of what any doctor said, that Randy would be walking again. Of course, he would–in no time at all.

Four months later, with no improvement at all, it was hard to remain optimistic.

"Why did God let this happen?" A.J. wanted to know. "Dad never hurt anybody. He was the best father in the world. Why would God do something like this to him?"

"God didn't do it, A.J.," I told him. "Don't ever blame things like strokes or any fatal disease or accident on the Lord. We don't understand why bad things happen to good people. Why did Grandma get cancer at the age of fifty-three and die? Why did Billy get killed by that drunk driver last summer? God allows things to happen. But He doesn't *make* them happen." I shook my head slowly. "We may never know the reason He lets human events take their own course. But there is one."

"God needed Grandma and Billy with Him," A.J. insisted. "But Dad's stuck on Earth, a prisoner in his own body! He's paralyzed! He can't even talk right anymore! He can't ever go fishing or boating or four-wheeling or anything!"

"A.J.," I said softly, trying to calm him down. "Do not blame God. Dad can get well with therapy."

"No, he won't!" A.J. shouted. "He'll *never* get better! It's been four months, and I don't see anything improving!

He can't ever go hunting with me again! He can't show me the easy way to clean catfish! He can't wrestle me to the ground! He can't cut wood with me or barbecue steaks on the grill or do anything fun! It's not fair!"

My son could not be comforted. He punched a hole in a wall, drove the riding lawnmower at full speed through the field and ruined it, and then went out with his friends and got drunk for the first time. Thank God he let a *sober* friend drive him home. He said he was thinking about Billy and decided he couldn't live with himself if he ever killed another person.

A few months later, at the beginning of A.J.'s senior year in high school, a Marine recruiter came to the school on career day. It might have been the uniform that impressed A.J. so much. Or maybe it was the confidence and presence the Marine possessed. Whatever the cause, the recruiter convinced my son that he simply had to be a Marine.

Randy and I thought it was a passing thing . He would never follow through with such a crazy idea. Marines were barbaric, weren't they? A.J. would never survive boot camp, let alone getting constantly yelled at. Reality wasn't like the Gomer Pyle show we'd watched as kids.

Besides, we had plenty of time to talk A.J. out of it. He had to be eighteen, and he had just turned seventeen. Surely, a year would make a big difference.

And that it did. He became even more determined. So determined that he joined the delayed-enlistment program and began to train for boot camp.

Randy and I signed the papers. By then, it was clear we weren't going to talk him out of it. But we did, at least, try to talk him into joining an easier branch of the service. Randy and I had met in the Air Force, so we tried getting A.J. to talk to an Air Force recruiter. Options are important, we said. A.J. didn't want options. He had his heart set on being a Marine–one of the few, the proud. Nothing was going to stop him.

I will never forget the day Darin and I went to the Hilton in Fort Smith, to be a part of a welcome program for parents of future Marines. We walked into the hotel conference room and took our seats on the left side, with the families and siblings of the recruits. The very few recruits. I was a surprised at how few there were.

They served a great lunch and had a wonderful program explaining the advantages of being part of such an elite branch of the service. The non-commissioned officers stood in formation according to rank. Glances across the room at my son told me that A.J. was awed by what years of dedication could bring him.

Afterward, still confused about the low attendance of new recruits, I asked A.J, "Why aren't there more people here? I see maybe thirty of you guys. That's all they recruited from half the state of Arkansas in an entire month?"

A.J.'s eyes grew wide, and he grabbed his red Marine T-shirt. "Mom!" he admonished, "this is the United States Marines! They don't want just *anybody*."

No, I guess they didn't. But they did want my son.

September 11, 2001. Who among us will ever forget it?

Like most of America–like most of the *world*–our family was glued to the television screen. A.J. had a look on his face I had never seen before as he watched the plane plummet into the second of the Twin Towers, then both Towers tumble helplessly to the Earth.

Standing in front of our fifty-two-inch Toshiba, teeth clenched and his gaze hard and cold, he muttered, "No way. Damn it! They can't get away with this!"

I thought the terrible disaster would change his mind about joining the Marines. It wasn't quite official yet. He could still have backed out, as I reminded him. I knew in my heart that there would be a war, that America would not simply turn the other cheek and let those who'd perpetrated that evil act go unpunished. That was the straw that broke the Nation's back. The idea that my son could end up in the middle of the war that was to come made my blood run cold.

A.J. didn't change his mind about enlisting after 9-11. In fact, he was more determined than ever to do it—more eager to defend our country. And despite my fear for his safety, I admit, I shared his enthusiasm. I wished I were eighteen again and could be part of something like the Marines. I was proud of my son and his strong convictions and patriotism.

I was proud, too, that he made it through the strict tests that allowed him to follow his dream. After all, he'd had a broken femur when he was three years old, and his eyesight wasn't perfect by a long shot. As the doctor had warned us, the concussion had affected his optical nerve, and sometimes A.J.'s vision was no better than 20/70. Luckily, his eye test came on a good day; 20/40 was passing without corrective lenses, and he passed. The Marines would never know that A.J.'s eyes couldn't be corrected *with* lenses and that he would always have trouble with his vision.

Three days after high school graduation, A.J. turned eighteen. The next day, he was sent to boot camp, in San Diego, where he would have to endure thirteen weeks of the same kind of training given to Navy Seals.

I used to jog with A.J. to help motivate him into shape. I wondered if those five miles a day, which was all I could manage, would help him get through the average of *fifteen* miles a day that would be required of him. I wondered if his feelings were getting hurt when he was yelled at. I wondered if the food was good and what they were feeding them. I wondered how much sleep he was getting and how much endurance they expected of these young people.

I thought about A.J.'s grades in high school. He had been a solid *B* student. But he told me that the Marines weren't impressed by good grades and didn't care whether or not a recruit was smart. All that mattered was his physical condition and if he had all his fingers and toes. Having some familiarity with the military myself, I knew that intelligence did matter–eventually. Just not in boot camp.

I didn't get an address for A.J. for two weeks. Didn't they realize that these teenagers needed mail? My first letter from A.J. arrived nineteen days after he'd gone and consisted of two sentences: *I'll write more later when they give us time. So far they've been total assholes.*

His first few letters after that were filled with complaints and aggravation. Then I began to notice a change. He started talking about confidence, perseverance, integrity, pride, and indomitable spirit.

His brothers and I, along with several aunts and

uncles and cousins, went to his graduation on August 30, 2002. Randy wanted badly to go with us, but he and I agreed it would have proven nearly impossible for him; he was simply too uncomfortable traveling more than a few miles. Still, A.J. had quite an audience, and the Marines put on quite a show for us.

They were unbelievable as they marched perfectly in formation, appearing like row after row of clones. How would I find my son, I wondered, among all those recruits? They all had the same hair, the same uniform, even the same body, for heaven's sake!

We found A.J.'s company (India) and platoon number (#3691) on a sign and examined each Marine individually. Finally, I spotted him, and, naturally, I yelled his name at the top of my lungs and waved, just like a mom. He flashed that famous Allen smile, which served to reassure me entirely that, far from being a clone, he was still my son. Still my A.J.

I had never understood men when they said they were so proud, the buttons popped off their shirts. Watching my son do that final march as a Marine recruit, I came to understand. I have never been prouder of anyone in my entire life.

The first words out of his mouth when we finally met were, "Mom! Tell me a story!"

And so I did. Everyone listened as I repeated a favorite of A.J.'s.

"A.J. always gave me an itemized summary of how much his report cards were worth, depending on the grade. For example, an A was worth five dollars, B's were worth three dollars, and so forth. He was in the second grade and handed me his report card. There, next to each grade was a total amount due. I studied it. He had two D's. Next to the D's, he wrote fifty cents each. I was surprised that he thought he would get paid for a grade below average, and I asked him why he thought he should get fifty cents for the D's. He responded with, "Oh! They're not worth very much."

Everyone roared, so I added, "How much was this thirteen weeks worth, A.J?"

He said without hesitation, "No money this time, Mom. I'd do it all again just to see the look on your face when you first saw me. It was priceless. You were so puffed up!"

I wasn't alone, though. All the families who'd come to watch the ceremony were beaming. They were people of all ages and from all walks of life. They'd traveled from as far away as Ohio and Florida, some packed into beat–up old pickups, others in Corvettes and Mercedes. The occupants included old men and women all the way down to babies. I felt like they spent their last dollar to see that precious loved one graduate from such an elite branch of the military.

Bottom line, it didn't matter where you came from. It didn't matter if your parents graduated from Yale, Mesa College in Grand Junction, Colorado, or just made it through high school. It didn't matter what they did in their life. They had a reason to be proud now. They were watching something that happens once in a lifetime. Their loved one was now a United States Marine.

They say, 'Once a Marine, always a Marine.' I truly believe that.

It was incredible to me to witness such pride in the American people.

In those young men and women, we were witnessing the very best of what America stands for. No one Marine was better than another. Regardless of where they had come from, or how rich or poor their families were, they were all equal in their new roles as defenders of our country. They represented perseverance, honor, self-control, integrity, and patriotism.

The Pledge of Allegiance had never rung so true in my heart as it did that day. We said it together, all of us—parents and grandparents, sons and daughters, civilians and Marines—united in mind and spirit. And I can still hear the sound of freedom in those words. I knew then, as I had never known before, that we are, indeed, "one nation under God, indivisible, with liberty and justice for all."

That's what a Marine stands for. Never forget it.

After the graduation ceremony, A.J. introduced us to his new friend, Mason. Of course, we knew that was his last name. They all referred to A.J. as Allen.

Mason's family and ours stood together, listening, as our new Marines described the last thirteen weeks of "pure hell" for our benefit.

Mason had been given an especially tough lesson in "show no fear." He was afraid of heights, and they'd all been required to bungee jump from a tower two hundred feet high.

"I'll tell you, ma'am," he said to me, "I was shaking in my boots, watching the line in front of me get shorter and shorter."

"You should have seen the look his face, Mom, when they hooked him up to the bungee cord. He was about to puke."

Mason shook his head. "It's true, I was sure I was going to lose it. Then, when I got the command to jump, I just froze up solid. No way was I going to take my feet off that concrete platform. The sergeant tried to reason with me, explained I might end up in a situation someday where I'd have to jump into thin air to survive. And the guys all called me baby and wimp and every name in the book that I can't repeat in ladies' company to get me to go. But it didn't matter. I just wasn't going to do it."

"What finally changed your mind?" I asked, knowing he had to have jumped eventually, or he wouldn't have graduated.

A.J. laughed. "Let's say his mind got changed *for* him."

"They pushed me, ma'am," Mason said. "And I reckon the entire population of San Diego heard me screaming."

"You mean, the entire population of California, don't you?" A.J. corrected.

"You got over your fear in just one jump?" I asked him.

Mason and A.J. looked at one another, then burst out laughing.

"No, ma'am," he said politely. "They made me jump over ten times–until I stopped screaming."

The boy was absolutely charming. In fact, I didn't meet a Marine that day that wasn't. They were all friendly and self-deprecating and polite to a fault. And they were so clearly proud of their accomplishment, of having gotten through a grueling ordeal and achieved their goal.

A.J. was stationed at Camp LeJeune in North

Carolina. His MOS (Military Occupational Specialty) was No. 1371, Combat Engineer. Being a new private, he was eager to explain his job to me.

"We build fighting holes, bunkers...you know, Mom—foxholes. We also build bridges, and we specialize in demolition and construction. There are only about forty of us, and we're the only bridge company in the Marine Corps. We just built a bunch of bridges that'll hold seventy-ton vehicles and last for 10,000 passes. They're medium-girder bridges that'll span a hundred and sixty-two-foot gap."

I was impressed. I looked up "MOS 1371 Combat Engineer" and read the official job description: "Combat engineers construct, alter, repair, and maintain buildings and structures; lift and move heavy objects and equipment by setting up, bracing, and utilizing rigging devices and equipment, and perform various duties incidental to the use of demolitions in construction projects and destruction of objects. Personnel assigned this MOS are taught carpentry and other construction skills as well as demolitions, specialized demolitions for urban breaching, and land-mine warfare."

The requirements for the job included an MM (rifle) score of 95 or higher.

A.J. told me his eyesight was at its worst the day he had to do the rifle test. The weather didn't help, as it was raining heavily. He could only miss two out of fifteen hits at the target and pass, and after he missed the first one, he realized he would never pass this test. He could hardly see the target.

"I just stood there and knew I couldn't do it," he told me over the phone. "I was dripping wet and miserable, and all I could think was, 'I've come all this way for nothing because, now, they'll know. Now, they'll find out how bad my eyes are, and they'll kick me out.' And all I could think to do was pray. So I asked God to help me." He gave a short laugh. "I *begged* Him to help me. And He came through. I have no idea how I did it–I still couldn't see the damned target through all that rain and with my eyes like they were. All I could do was point the rifle in the right direction and leave the aiming up to the Lord. I missed two, but I got the ninety-five I needed to pass."

Through the tears choking my throat, I smiled and said, "Well, I'm not surprised. You and God have made a pretty good team for a long time, now."

I reminded myself of that when A.J. called to tell us that he was being sent to Kuwait.

"None of us have any idea what to expect," he said.

"Will you be building bridges?" I asked.

"The bridges have already been built. They were sent to Kuwait on pallets, and we'll be assembling them once we get there."

He sounded so confident, so determined. And yet...

"Are you scared, A.J.?" I asked. My own heart was pounding in my chest, and my hands were like ice, both clutching the phone receiver.

"Yes," he admitted. "I'm scared. You'd be a fool not to be, I guess."

"Do you regret joining the Marines?"

"No. I want America to stay free, Mom, and the only way to make sure we get to keep our freedom is to end the terrorism."

It was incredible to hear such grown-up words

coming from my child. I had to remember that A.J. wasn't a little boy anymore. He was a man.

"Where, exactly, will you be in Kuwait?" I asked, though I feared I already knew the answer.

His reply confirmed my suspicion.

"We're the tip of the arrow, Mom."

I had to swallow several times before I could speak again. And there was only one thing left to say.

"Have I told you lately that I love you, son?"

"Not today!" he said, and I could tell by his tone that he was smiling.

"I love you way past the Milky Way," I said trying to duplicate his cheerful attitude.

"Is that higher than Heaven?" he asked.

I chuckled, but I was thinking, *I'm not about to love you all the way to Heaven, not when I'm so afraid of losing you to it.*

"Can you do me a favor when you write me, Mom?"

"Name it," I managed to say.

"You know how I always love the stories you tell about me? The funny things I said and did that weren't funny when I did them but are now?"

"I know what you mean."

"Can you put some of those stories in your letters, so it feels more like home? Mom, are you there?"

"Yeah," I said, glad he couldn't see the tears streaming down my face.

Trying to regain my composure, I added, "Sure, I'll do it. I love to reminisce about your mischievous antics."

"My friend, Mason...actually he's my best friend now...he thinks it's crazy that you can remember so much. He says you must have a computer for a brain."

"Not a computer. A pen. I wrote things down when you said or did them and even dated the little paper I'd written them on. I have an entire shoebox full of things you kids have said and done that I never want to forget."

"I knew I had a smart mom."

"Darn right."

"You won't forget to put the stories in your letters?"

"Of course, I won't forget."

"Good. Now, I gotta go."

"Semper Fi!" I said. "And I love you higher than the stars!"

"Love you, too, Mom."

When I hung up the phone, I immediately went to retrieve my shoebox out the top of my bedroom closet. Taking it to the kitchen table, along with pen and paper, I began to write A.J. his first letter. I knew it would be a couple weeks before I'd have a mailing address for him, but I planned to write every day, regardless.

Sorting through the shoebox, I made a small pile of A.J.-related stories. Then I began to write:

Dear A.J.,

How's my favorite Marine in the whole wide world?

I just got off the phone with you and couldn't help but write my first letter. I don't know when I'll hear from you, but I wanted you to know this: Not a day will go by that you won't get a letter from me.

Have I told you lately that I love you? Just FYI.

I got the shoebox out and started going through all the little pieces of paper with my "sayings" scribbled on them. Here's a few to make you smile. (drum roll, please)

Age three–You had a headache.   You said, "Mom! My brain is hot!"

Age four–I told you that you needed to say please *when you wanted something.   You said, "If I say* please *one more time, my throat will hurt."*

Age four–You told me you were going to have a great big piece of the chocolate cake I just made.   You said, "Mom! I'm going to spoil my stomach real big!"

Age five–You were taking off your sweater.   It was winter and you had a T-shirt on underneath. The sweater was full of static. You exclaimed, "Mom! There's thunder in my shirt!"

Age five–You picked up my sunglasses and said you knew how to clean them. I asked how. You said, "You just yawn on them."

Age six–You were chewing your gum funny. I asked you why. You said, "My square tooth isn't as strong as the triangle one."

Age six–I asked you to turn off the light in the play room. You said, "How can I turn off the light when I'm scared stiff?"

Age seven–You asked, "Mom?   What is God's last name?" I said, "Well, God doesn't have a last name because He's the only one named God." You were quiet for a long time. Then you said, "Well, then, how does He get His mail?"

Age seven–We went for a long walk.   You stopped and took off one shoe and sock and began rubbing your toes. I asked what was wrong. You said, "My foot has a bunch of little dots in it!" (Your foot was asleep)

Age eight–You were always very good about saying your nightly prayers, and I always loved listening to you from the doorway without your knowing. One night you were really tired and mumbled something, then jumped into bed. Curious, I went in your room and said, "A.J. I didn't hear you say your prayers tonight." You responded, "That's because I told God it was the same one as last night."

I know you've heard these all a million times but thought you'd like to hear them again for old times' sake. It makes me smile when I read them because I remember exactly the moments they happened. I would grab anything handy to write on and jot them down, so this shoebox is full of everything from cake mix box lids to scraps of wrapping paper. One day I will write a book and put all these little stories in it. Then you'll be famous!

I want you to know how very proud I am of you, and of all the young men and women serving with you. You're all putting your lives on the line to protect the rest of us and the precious liberties our ancestors worked so hard to secure. I'm sure I speak for all Americans when I say we are truly grateful and honored.

Oh! And I keep forgetting to tell you this. I love you!

Marcie still thinks you're somewhere around, even though it's been months since you left home. She looks in your room and jumps on your bed that never needs to be re-made. She got used to sleeping with a human being and has adopted Darin in your absence! Darin's very good to her, but even he knows he's just a substitute.

She's definitely your dog.

Your dad has decided to quit physical therapy. He doesn't feel like it's doing him any good and wants to take a break. He promised he'll keep up with his exercises, so, under that condition, we agreed to let him stop. He says it's too hard, and he needs time to do it on his own. He's always been a couch potato. But don't worry. We won't let him get lazy. We hope he'll be walking, like old times, by the time you come home again.

Your sweet little girlfriend, Angela, called me a few minutes ago. She wants to come over and have me show her how to make salsa. I gave her a jar of some I made, and she loved it. I can't wait to see her. After all, she might be my daughter-in-law someday. You sure can pick them, A.J. She's a peach.

Bo says all he does is study and work, study and work. I keep telling him, that's what it takes! He's still amazed that his little brother is a Marine. He says he wouldn't have made it through the first week of boot camp. After Mason told us the height story, Bo told me his biggest phobia. Are you ready? Spiders! He said he figured the Marines might put him in a tank packed with tarantulas to make him get over it. He said it gave him the creeps just thinking about it.

Darin says his biggest fear is of clowns. Can you imagine? What do you think the Marines would do about that? Get a bunch of clowns together and have them tickle him to death? I'd like your opinion on this one.

Well, this is letter #1. I am marking each one so you'll know the order to read them if you get two or three in one day. I hope I made you laugh. I hope you know how much I love you. I hope you know that there's not a parent out there with more pride in her son than me.

God bless you and keep you always. My prayers are with you and all those who defend our country. Be safe, my dear one.

Love you way past the Big Dipper!
Mom

My Son is a Marine

THREE

It was several weeks before we got our first letter from A.J. The first thing he told us was how happy he'd been the first day of mail call to get five letters from me and how much they reminded him of home.

He talked about the food and living conditions. Being in a foreign country for the first time, he'd had no idea what to expect. It was spring in Kuwait, so the weather was very tolerable. The war had not been announced yet, but the troops were being kept busy with preparations.

I was especially moved by this particular section of A.J.'s letter:

Mom, I have to tell you this! We've had plenty of time to ourselves since we're in this waiting mode, and I've become pretty close to all my buddies. You hear me talk about them all the time. Gurule, Harrison, Happenstahl, Logan, Dunning, and, of course, Mason. We talk about everything. It turns out that Mason and Dunning don't believe in God! Can you imagine? The others believe but have a lot of questions about the whole concept. How could anyone possibly get through life without Him in it?

I had no idea how many people don't understand the full scope of what Jesus did for us. They think of Christmas with Santa Claus and Easter with the Energizer bunny! I had a lot of tough questions thrown at

me, especially from Mason.   He said he could not
understand why a father would send his son to die for a
bunch of people who didn't care.   After all, He was
condemned by His own people.

I never encountered anything like this before. I told
them the bird story you always told us as kids. It left them
thinking.   Did I do the right thing or should I have
explained it using the Bible? Just wondering.

I reread that part of the letter twice. The bird story
was one of A.J.'s favorites. It's about a man of little faith
who tries to keep a flock of small birds from freezing
during a blizzard by opening his barn door to allow them
inside. When they don't take the hint, he tries leading
them with a path of seeds, but they still won't follow him.
Distraught and frustrated, the man shouts at the birds,
"What do I have to do to get you to understand me?
Become one of you?" And God answers him, *"Yes, that*
is what I had to do. That is why I sent My Son. He had to
be trusted and lead the way, or all of you would have
died."

In the letter I wrote to A.J. that day, I assured him
that he was doing the right thing in bearing witness to the
Lord and being open about his faith with his friends. But
I also told him that faith wasn't something you could *give*
to another human being. It was something each person
had to find on his or her own.

As I wrote, I was deeply grateful that A.J. had found
his path to the Lord a long time ago, and that his faith had
had many years to grow strong and sure. I was deeply
afraid that he was going to need not only his physical
might but every ounce of spiritual strength he possessed

in the days to come.

It was March 19, 2003. I was in Wal-Mart with my eighty-eight-year-old great-aunt. We stopped in front of a bank of televisions, all showing what appeared to be live coverage of bombings taking place. An instant later, the announcer said we were watching the bombing of Iraq.

It was a shocking sight. I held on to my frail old aunt, and we cried together. I couldn't remember seeing anything so devastating as all that smoke, knowing my son was smack dab in the middle of it.

The rest of the day was a blur. I went home and glued myself to the television. A.J. and I had talked about the possibility of war. I asked him if he thought the rest of the world was as concerned as we were. He said that they should be and then for once in his life, *he told me a story*. As memory serves, it goes like this:

A mouse looked through a crack in the wall to see the farmer and his wife opening a package and wondered what food it might contain. He was mortified to see that it was a mousetrap!

He ran swiftly to the farmyard and proclaimed the warning, *'There's a mousetrap in the house! There's a mouse trap in the house!'*

The chicken clucked and scratched and raised her head and said, *"Mr. Mouse, I can tell you this is a serious concern for you but it's of no consequence to me. I can't be bothered by it."*

The mouse turned to the pig and told him the same thing...that there was a mousetrap in the house.

The pig replied, *"I'm so very sorry, Mr. Mouse. But there's nothing I can do about it. Tell ya what. I'll pray for you."*

The mouse turned to the cow and told him the same thing...that there was a mousetrap in the house.

The cow continued to chew and act non-chalant. He said, *"So what? A mousetrap? Ooooh! Like I'm in grave danger!"*

The little mouse was devastated and returned to the house with his head down. He felt totally rejected and decided to face the farmer's mousetrap on his own.

That very night a sound was heard throughout the house. It was the sound of a mousetrap catching its prey. The farmer's wife rushed to see what was caught.

It was dark and she didn't know that a venomous snake had his tail caught in the trap. It bit the farmer's wife. The farmer rushed his wife to the hospital. She returned home with a fever.

Now everyone knows you treat a fever with fresh chicken soup so the farmer took his hatchet and killed the chicken for the soup's main ingredient.

The farmer's wife continued to get sicker so that friends and neighbors had to sit with her around the clock. The farmer butchered the pig to feed them all.

Well, the farmer's wife died and so many people came to the funeral that the farmer had to slaughter his cow to provide meat for all of them to eat.

The next time you hear someone is facing a problem. Don't think it doesn't concern you. Remember when the least of us is threatened, we are all at risk.

War. I'd known it was coming. But seeing it–live, no less–was even worse than I had imagined it would be. I was terrified for my son, as well as for every other mother's son. Besides that, I was struck by the dramatic and permanent changes being wrought so far away from my own safe home. The face of the world was changing before my very eyes, and I knew this war would affect many thousands of lives.

The days dragged on with no word from my son.

I continued to write every day, and I always included little stories in each letter. I also always dedicated at least two paragraphs to Marcie's latest antics.

A.J. had taught her to trap snakes. If she caught a copperhead, he would kill it, but in the case of king or other beneficial snakes, he would make her back off so the snake was free to go.

I had a hard letter to write when Marcie was bitten by a cottonmouth at our pond. Cottonmouths are very venomous, even more so than copperheads. Marcie was extremely sick, and the vet wasn't optimistic about her chances. There wasn't much we could do for her. We nursed her as the vet had instructed and hoped for the best.

For two weeks, I kept A.J. informed of her daily progress. As I wrote those letters, I kept remembering the conversation he and I had had shortly before he left for boot camp.

"Mom, are there dogs in Heaven?" he'd asked me.

I laughed. "You tell me. You're the one who's been there, remember?"

A.J. chuckled. "I guess I was too busy to look around much. But your opinion."

"Well, I've heard that people who've had experiences similar to yours claim they've seen horses and dogs in

Heaven. Personally, I think anything you loved could be there."

"Anything you loved. Hmm..." He scooped up Marcie in his arms, hugging her. "So, uh, you think, say, an opossum could make it?"

I looked at him with disapproval. "I doubt it. But..." I shrugged. "Who knows? If it was a pet and you really loved it, why not? Don't we take love with us when we go?"

A.J. stared at Marcie a long time before answering. "It can't be bad where they go. In fact, if there aren't any dogs in Heaven, then when I die, I want to go where they go."

Whoever said that praying over an animal was a waste of time? Before Marcie's snake crisis, I had laid my hands on other pets and prayed, and I don't think it did any harm.

Marcie was no different. Except that I wasn't praying for her sake as much as I was for A.J.'s. I asked the Lord to heal Marcie, because my son loved and cherished her.

It seemed, though, that my prayers were in vain. Marcie drifted into a coma and wasn't expected to make it through the night. I prayed very hard, but knew in my heart that she was gone.

Wondering how I was going to write that day's letter to A.J., I went to the animal clinic early the next morning. I planned to tell the vet to take Marcie off the respirator and let her die in peace. But something incredible had happened during the night. Just when I had given up, Marcie had decided to start fighting for her life.

I walked into the clinic to find a very weak, very thin Jack Russell, wagging her little stubby tail and begging for something to eat. The veterinarian said he had never seen anything like it. It was truly a miracle.

I thought so, too, and that's what I told A.J. when I wrote to him that afternoon.

To keep from spending every waking hour worrying about A.J., Randy's continued lack of improvement, and our dwindling savings, I filled my days by focusing on positive things that I knew would make a difference.

I wrote pieces for our local newspaper filled with news from Iraq, firsthand accounts taken from A.J.'s letters. As a result of the articles, our local radio station interviewed me a couple of times. I was happy to have the chance, both through the newspaper and the radio, not only to give people accurate information about what was going on but also to ask them to pray for our troops.

Our town organized a rally– "Support Our Soldiers Overseas" –to be held at the city park. The mayor spoke. A DJ played music, and people danced. T-shirts, hats, and yellow ribbons were sold to collect money in support of our troops.

As the mother of the "hometown boy" in Iraq, I was asked to speak, too.

After introducing myself, I emphasized the importance of supporting our troops. I focused on prayer and the fact that it is the most powerful force on Earth.

"President Bush is Commander–in–Chief and he depends on prayer. He asks every American to pray for our nation, our troops and him," I said. "He's earned the respect and admiration of these troops. We should take a picture of all of us here right now…including everyone we know and love and send it to every single soldier fighting this war. Then tell them *'This is who you are fighting for. Thank you!'*

"Let me ask you a question. If the troops could just see one rally on TV right now, what would you like them to see? How about us? Wouldn't it be great for them to see this rally here today? Look at all of you who came here to show your support! We are *soooo* proud of them! Every soldier has to take an oath before they are official. They must raise their right hand and promise to *'protect the United States of America'* and that's what they are doing."

Next, I tried to paint a picture for the crowd of what life was like for those brave young men and women fighting for America.

"They carry a seventy-pound pack that holds everything they own on their backs, at all times," I told them. "They wear combat boots that rarely leave their feet because they have to be prepared for anything. They haven't had a shower in weeks, and they're probably wearing the same underwear and socks for that long, too. They're lucky to get five hours of sleep in a twenty-four-hour period. They live outside in any kind of weather. They eat C-rations, and their only beverage is water."

I looked at the quiet, somber crowd spread out before me, but in my mind's eye, what I saw, as I continued to speak, was my son's face. "These young people are thousands of miles from home, in a hostile country. They are experiencing the dangers of a battle unlike any we've ever seen before. They know their fate if they're captured or ambushed, and they're in a constant state of alertness. Yes, they've been trained, and trained well. My son told me every Marine has been given two syringes to inject themselves with, if they're exposed to nerve gas." Seeing the shocked, horrified looks, I nodded. "That's right. Nerve gas. They *expect* things like that to happen. They're ready for it. Their motto is: *"We do whatever it takes to secure our freedom."*

"The rules of war have changed. These soldiers have to worry that the man approaching them in a uniform just like their own could be the enemy–and that he might be wired with explosives and prepared to blow himself up to kill them. If he's driving a vehicle just like theirs, they have to worry that he's a suicide bomber and that the truck or jeep has been rigged to blow up."

I went on for some time, telling my listeners about the horrific things A.J. had related to me. I told them, too, about the friendship and loyalty that had grown among the troops.

Finally, I used the golden opportunity the rally presented to convey the same message I'd tried to convey in my newspaper articles and radio interviews:

"In A.J.'s last letter to me before the war was announced, he asked us all to pray for them. And I know that many of you are doing just that. For those of you who aren't, please think about this: These are critical times, times when we need our faith in God more than ever. It doesn't matter what words you use. It only matters that those words are sincere. If you speak from the heart, your prayer will travel to Heaven like a little flicker of light and be seen.

"When we unite and pray together, though, well, that's when we really shake things up. Group prayer is a powerful thing–like a lightning bolt that illuminates all of Heaven.

"So let's pray together now–as one nation under God, indivisible. Let's ask the Almighty to look after all those brave souls who are fighting for us–and for freedom– thousands of miles away."

A.J. was assigned to the 8th ESB, 2nd platoon, "C" Company. He informed me that boxes soldiers received were all shared among the entire platoon. An area at the back of the tent was set aside for things people had sent, and any soldier could help him or herself to whatever was needed.

A.J. sent a list of the things they needed most and asked me to pass the word to everyone I knew. The list included antibacterial baby wipes, gallon-size storage bags, cotton swabs, pre-sweetened drink mixes, black socks (all sizes), foot powder, shoe liners with baking soda, beef jerky, candy, Chapstick, sunscreen, tightie underwear, all sizes of batteries, and...ice. (That last item made me laugh, but I knew those kids weren't laughing, sitting in the 140-degree desert).

I made copies of the list and started handing it out everywhere I went. A lot of people asked me questions: Why would a soldier need baby wipes or plastic Zip-loc bags? Because, I explained at least a million times, many of the places our troops were stationed in Iraq had no electricity and no water, so taking a bath or doing laundry was virtually impossible. So the baby wipes were an improvised "shower in a tube," and the socks were replacements for ones the soldiers wore until they were rags and ready to be thrown out. Generous use of foot powder kept them from getting athlete's foot in the meantime.

Aside from the lack of water, sand was the biggest problem. It blew unmercifully and got into every crevice of everything that wasn't sealed in plastic–hence, the plastic storage bags. And, since sand also had a way of burrowing beneath clothing to fill belly buttons, ears, nostrils, and the cracks between fingers and toes, tightie underwear helped to keep it out of the more delicate parts of the anatomy.

With the necessities of life taken care of, the troops also loved to get snacks. Beef jerky was a big favorite because it didn't spoil. They liked getting candy, too, although A.J. said they gave most of it away to Iraqi children.

Thanks to the support of many of my friends and neighbors and our church congregation, A.J.'s platoon received over fifty "care packages," at least thirty of which were from the local schools. A.J. told me his platoon was overwhelmed by the support and generosity everyone had shown.

I was, too. I can hardly express how it felt to know that I was not the only one thinking about my son and his comrades. I wasn't the only one doing what little an ordinary American could do to take care of those kids, so far away. And I wasn't the only one praying with all my might, asking the Lord, please, to take care of all those young people and to see them safely home again.

My Son is a Marine

FOUR

Money was getting uncomfortably low. Randy's disability checks weren't nearly enough to cover the bills. I had depleted much of our savings and had begun to dip into my retirement fund.

What had happened to my great plan? The one where Randy would be walking by now and taking care of himself. He was always able to do transfers, but living without the wheelchair was the main goal. If that was achieved then I would be able to go back to work. And we *all* would be able to have a life again.

As it was, Randy could not even pour himself a glass of orange juice.

I admit I was frustrated by his lack of progress. I'd signed up for "in sickness and in health," but...well, I'm human. My patience had run out. I wanted to crawl inside Randy's incapacitated body and *make* him do the things I thought he should be able to do. In the beginning, right after his stroke, he'd made such good progress. But since he'd quit physical therapy, he seemed to be taking one step forward and two back.

Worse, his mental health was suffering, as well. He acted as if he simply didn't care anymore whether he ever improved.

"Reach down! Reach way down there, and pull up your bootstraps," I told him. "Show the boys and me that you aren't going to give up! You're only forty-eight. You have a lot of years left on this Earth. Do you want to spend them all in that wheelchair?"

"No," he'd reply–sometimes. Other times, he just sighed. Those sighs scared me and made me all the more frustrated.

"Go back to therapy," I said to him. "It's all covered by insurance. Or, if you really can't stand going, at least follow the exercises they gave you. Do *something*! The boys and I love you, Randy, and we know you can do it!"

Whether or not he could, he didn't. I found the exercise sheets from the physical therapist wadded up in the trash.

And so the days dragged on. I took the phone with me wherever I went and kept the line open all the time. The stress of waiting for A.J. to call and watching my husband's health and spirit plummet took its toll on me. I know I aged at least five years in the course of just a few months.

Then the air-conditioner broke, and a new compressor cost over fourteen hundred dollars. Next, one of the big trees beside our house died and started dropping large limbs on the yard and the house, and it had to be taken down. If that weren't enough, the washing machine did its last load of laundry, and we had to invest in another one. Consequently, my credit card debt skyrocketed.

I felt more overwhelmed than I had ever felt in my life. So overwhelmed that, I admit, I was beginning to wonder if God had deserted me.

I reached the end of my rope the day Randy lost control of his bowels. It was early, and I was in the kitchen, making coffee. I heard him cry out, and, at first, I thought he'd fallen. I ran toward the bathroom and, when I saw what had happened, came to a dead halt.

He had obviously been trying to get to the toilet. The trail of his progress started at the bed in our room and ended three feet shy of the goal.

I called Darin to get up and help me, and he appeared almost instantly. I saw the shock on his face, but he didn't say a word.

He just supported his father, lifting him as necessary as I began to remove my husband's soiled clothing. I threw everything but his shoes into the trash.

Randy kept apologizing, and I kept saying it was all right. But in fact, it wasn't okay. It wasn't okay at all. Things were getting worse and worse, and I could see that it was only a matter of time—and not very much time—before I wouldn't be capable of taking care of him.

Together, Darin and I gave Randy a shower, got him dressed again, and back into his bleach-cleaned wheelchair. Then, leaving Darin to fix Randy breakfast, I picked up the trashcan of soiled clothing and took it outside.

Living on a farm, we were allowed to burn our trash. The burning barrel was located a good ways from the house. Dousing the clothes with gas, I threw them into the barrel and lit them. As the flames shot upward, I lost control of my senses and began to scream.

I screamed as loudly as I could. I wanted God to hear me.

"I can't do this! I'm not a nurse! I have a husband who doesn't care anymore whether he lives or dies! I have a son in Iraq, and I don't know if he's dead or alive! And where are *You* while all this is happening? You said you only give us what we can handle! That's Your promise! Well, You've overdone it this time! I can't handle this! I feel like I'm in prison here! I hate what I'm doing, and I hate that I can't change it, and I just hate everything about my life! I don't feel as if it will ever be good again! *Where are You?* Why can't I *feel* You? Why don't you *answer me*?"

I remained at the burning barrel, feeling sorry for myself, for over an hour.

When I finally went back to the house, I decided to write A.J. a letter. That always seemed to lift my spirits. I grabbed my "story shoebox" and headed for my office.

There, I sat at the desk and started shuffling through the shoebox, looking for "stories" that didn't already have a red X on them. Those were the ones I had used in previous letters. When I unfolded a piece of letter-size paper with typing on it, I stared at it, frowning. *Nothing* in this shoebox was typed.

"Who put this here?" I muttered under my breath. Quickly skimming the sheet, I saw that it wasn't about any of the boys. In fact, it wasn't any kind of personal note of mine.

I began to read the paper more closely.

A woman came to a beautiful tree growing in a lush, green valley. Hanging from one of the lower limbs, she saw a delicate cocoon blowing gently in the breeze. It had a small opening at one end, and through it, she could see the butterfly struggling to free itself from the prison.

She watched it for a long time, and she could see that the butterfly's body was much too big to fit through the tiny hole. When the butterfly seemed to give up, the woman was sad. Feeling sorry for it, she couldn't resist helping it escape.

She plucked the cocoon from the leaf and gently tore it open, smiling as she watched the butterfly emerge with great ease. But its body was very swollen, and the wings were small and shriveled. Patiently, she stood there, allowing the butterfly to crawl around on her hand and waiting for the wings to expand so they could support the butterfly's body. She expected, also, to see the body contract to normal size at any moment.

But nothing happened. The butterfly's wings dried out and spread, but they did not get any larger. Nor did its body shrink.

Then the Lord appeared next to the woman. The woman raised her gaze from the pitiful little butterfly to meet His.

"Why won't it fly?" she asked.

The Lord looked at the struggling butterfly.

"You thought you were doing a kindness," He said. "But you do not have nature's patience. The restricting cocoon and the struggle required for the butterfly to get through the tiny opening were nature's way of forcing fluid from the butterfly's body into its wings. Once it freed itself from the cocoon, it would have been ready for flight."

"I didn't know it was supposed to struggle," the woman said with regret heavy in her voice.

"Sometimes struggles are exactly what you need in your life," the Lord said. "If you were allowed to go through life without having to overcome obstacles, you would be as crippled as this butterfly."

When I finished reading the story, I hung my head and asked God to forgive me. I didn't even question how the story had gotten into my shoebox. Whether I'd stuck it there myself long ago without remembering, or whether the Lord had simply put it there Himself, was immaterial. It was quite obvious He had meant for me to find and read it at that moment in my life.

Who was I to feel sorry for myself? The struggles I was facing were put there to make me stronger. I needed to be strong for my husband, for my son still at home, for the one off at college...and especially for my son in Iraq.

Ashamed of myself, yet still feeling the weight of the burdens I was carrying, I spent the rest of the day preparing a birthday/care package for A.J. It seemed that the more love I packed into that box, the better I felt. It was great to feel positive again.

He was going to be nineteen on May 3. Just the thought of him opening the box made me smile. It included four batches of his favorite peanut butter cookies, a box of twenty birthday candles with one taken out, a homemade card that we all signed, a remnant of an old stuffed animal that Marcie had dissected, several Ping-Pong balls, a small photo album with various pictures of us all enjoying vacations, $1000 in Monopoly money, a pink disposable razor from my own supply (I knew he'd roll his eyes at that one, having warned me about sending embarrassing things–after I'd sent him a pair of Spiderman underpants from his elementary school days), and a box of tampons (used for plugging up wounds and for helmet and boot cushions).

I sent the package off, hoping A.J. would get it, if not on, at least close to his birthday.

The news was filled with stories of captured units, casualties, videos of smoke-filled skies, stories of suicide bombers, angry Iraqis wanting the Americans to go home, downed helicopters, warheads being shot into crowds of people, and the awful living conditions of our young men and women. I watched the news constantly, hoping for a glimpse of A.J. I worried about him constantly.

I worried about how he was holding up in the unbearable heat. I wanted to make him his favorite giant cheeseburger, with lots and lots of dill pickles. I wanted to pour him a glass of ice-cold Dr. Pepper and let him sit in our air-conditioned living room.

I worried, too, about his mental state, particularly if he'd had to kill anyone yet. It seemed a near-certainty that he would have to, although, being in an engineering unit, his job wasn't specifically to attack enemy forces. Still, this was war, where people killed other people, and I thought it was inevitable that A.J. would have to do the same, if only to defend himself. If...when...he did kill someone, would it haunt him for the rest of his life? Would he be different when he came home?

Would he come home? That question haunted me day and night. I had a ball of anxiety in the pit of my stomach, and it never went away.

The day we heard the afternoon news anchorman announce that the Eighth ESB Battalion had been captured, that knot in my stomach exploded in a rush of adrenaline that took over my entire being.

"*What*?" I cried, dropping the knife I'd been using to spread butter on a slice of bread and scrambling frantically for the volume control on the television. "Did he say the Army or the Marines? Did he say 'C' company? Everyone be quiet so I can hear!" Not that anyone was making any noise whatsoever. Randy and Darin were as riveted to the screen as I was.

But that was all the information we were given: The Eighth ESB Battalion.

"What exactly does that mean?" I exclaimed. "Are there a lot of these Eighth ESB Battalions?"

I called Bo, and he had heard the same thing. We all did what any normal family would do. We freaked out.

Twenty-four hours passed with no further word, just an overpowering dread and feeling of helplessness. Then, suddenly, I realized that I hadn't even prayed. All I'd done was watch the television screen and worry.

Hadn't I just given a speech about the power of prayer? Why wasn't I practicing what I preached? I'd lost twenty-four hours of praying time. Worse, I'd given those hours to Satan. He loves it when we worry, because it shows how little faith we have. Worry is something a person with faith gives to God.

Yet again I had cause to be ashamed at how self-absorbed I'd become, and at how little attention I was giving to the needs of my soul. I immediately asked Randy and Darin to pray with me, and they readily agreed. Within a few hours, our minds were put at ease. A.J. and his battalion were safe. The unit that had been captured wasn't even remotely connected to his.

The next day, I wrote another article for the local paper. They published it on May 3, 2003:

Today is my son A.J.'s nineteenth birthday. We aren't having birthday cake and ice cream with him today. We aren't celebrating his birthday with him at all. He's a Private First Class in the United States Marines, and he's in Iraq, fighting a war.

Let me ask you this: What were you doing when you were nineteen? Were you in college? Did you yet have your first real job? Were you already married and starting a family? Or were you in a war in a foreign country, sleeping in foxholes, eating ten-year-old food packed with preservatives, and dreaming of taking a shower to get rid of the sand that had worked its way into every crevice of your body?

Maybe some of you were in a war, the one we were engaged in, in Vietnam. But for those who weren't and who have no idea what it means to be in the middle of a war on your nineteenth birthday, let me try to give you an idea.

It means you're not old enough to buy beer, but you're old enough to die for your country. You're not a kid anymore. You're a man or woman.

It means you have learned that your canteen must be full and your feet dry at all times. You can forget to brush your teeth, but you can never forget to clean your gun.

It means you might not remember a single poem you had to read in high school, but you can recite the nomenclature of a machine gun or grenade launcher and use both effectively.

It means you share food, water, and ammunition with other young men and women you've only recently met, but who have already become your best friends. Friends who might save your life the next day—or the next minute.

It means you've learned to put time into perspective. To realize the value of nine months, ask a mother who just gave birth to a stillborn baby. To realize the value of a second, ask someone who survived a near-fatal accident. To realize the value of a millisecond, ask someone who just won the silver medal in the Olympics.

To realize the value of a friend...lose one.

A.J. called three weeks after the article appeared. The caller ID showed the same odd area code that was always attached to his calls, so I knew it had to be him.

"Hello?" I said, nearly dropping the phone in my excitement.

A long pause ensued before I heard that familiar, beloved voice.

"Mom!"

"A.J.! My God! How are you?"

Another delay.

"Mom, listen—I've only got five minutes, and I need you to do something really important for me. I need you to tell me that dream you had about Jesus with you and me. Remember the one I'm talking about?"

"Yes, but—"

"I need to hear it right now, so start talking!"

A.J.'s tone was eerie, and his request—his demand, really—seemed most bizarre. Of all the things he could have said, he wanted me to tell him about a dream I'd had years ago, a dream he already knew quite well?

I'd hesitated less than five seconds, but it had been long enough to put a note of panic into his voice.

"Mom! It's important! Go!" he yelled.

Shaking as I thought about what might have driven A.J. to such lengths, I did as he asked. "You and I were the only ones walking through a crowded street," I began. "You were wearing a long lime-green robe, and I was wearing a cream-colored one. There were a lot of people, all wearing robes, but yours was the only one that weird shade of green.

"We were holding hands, so we wouldn't lose each

other, and we walked until we came to a large room. When we went inside, a man was speaking to a group of people, mostly men. He asked us all to sit down, and He put you about four feet from me. You were the only child. We sat on the floor with our legs crossed, Indian style. Then, the man sat down between you and me, but he was facing me. I realized then that he was Jesus. He looked right at me, square in the eyes, and smiled. Then He took His index finger and ran it down the bridge of my nose, saying, 'Jo Anne, your sins are forgiven.'

"Then He turned to you and said, 'A.J., remember this moment. The day will come when you will need me to do for you what I just did for your mother. You'll be given a burden that you'll find too heavy to carry by yourself. That moment will not belong to your mother, but she will share it with you.'"

Swallowing hard, I said, "That's it, A.J. That's the dream. Now, what's all this about?"

His voice was quivering when he replied. "I know this call is being monitored, but I don't care–I have to tell you. We were ambushed by a bunch of teenagers–kids like us, except younger. Mom, we...Sarge, Gurule, all of us...we had to shoot at them, and...and I killed one of them. I shot a *kid*, Mom! *A kid!*"

Dear God, please, tell me what to say to him.

"A.J., listen to me," I said. "You're in a war. I'm sure you–"

But he wasn't listening. "I can't sleep," he said. "I keep thinking about that dream–that green robe was the color I'm wearing now. Jesus *knew* I'd be in a war. He *knew* I'd kill somebody, and He knew I wouldn't be able to handle it! And He was right! I can't! I can't stand knowing I–"

"Honey, calm down! It's okay," I said, thinking fast. "Is there a chaplain there you can talk to–or someone you feel comfortable with?"

"I tried that," A.J. practically screamed. "It didn't help! All I can think about is that I might have to do it again–and that Jesus knew it when He gave you that dream. He *knew* I'd have to...to *kill people*." His voice cracked as he continued. "He was just a kid, like me, Mama, and he only had a knife. That's all any of them had–stupid little knives. But we thought they had bombs. We didn't know, so when they started attacking us, we just started shooting. Happenstahl got stabbed twice, and he's in the hospital, but those kids...they're all dead. Just...dead."

Feeling utterly helpless, I said, "It was self-defense, A.J. You could have been stabbed, too. You knew this could happen when you joined the Marines–and you *must* have known it would happen in a war. You had no choice, A.J. If you hadn't killed him, he would have killed you."

After a few seconds delay, he spoke again, no longer yelling, but in anguished tones. "It hurts so bad, Mama. I held him in my arms, and I felt...*so bad*. We were told to shoot, and I did, but...Mama, please, pray for me. Pray that it'll be all right."

"You know I will, A.J. I don't know how else to help you. But I want you to talk to the chaplain again, okay? Promise me you'll–"

There was a loud click on the line, followed by a dial tone. A.J. had used his five minutes.

I hung up the receiver and stood staring at it, my

heart aching for my son. I wished I could hold him and tell him everything would be okay. I wished this war had never happened. I wished I could go back and not sign the delayed-enlistment papers that had allowed A.J. to become a Marine.

Oh, *why* couldn't he have joined the Air Force? Then he wouldn't be on the front lines, where his life was in constant danger and he had to kill or be killed. He had three years to go, and the war was far from over. It was virtually inevitable that he would have to kill again. Would he be able to do it, or would his agony over the boy he'd killed make him hesitate—and end up getting *him* killed? Would he be tormented for the rest of his life by what he'd had to do in order to survive?

For that matter, why was he so tormented? At the same time my heart was breaking for my son, my brain was trying to make sense of his shock and horror at his own actions. He'd known what he was getting into. He talked solemnly and with clear understanding about the training he'd received in boot camp, the martial arts and kill techniques. Moreover, he'd known he would be on the front lines, where being attacked and shooting back was part of the normal course of war. Surely, he'd thought about that. Surely, he had expected to have to aim his gun and shoot it. Obviously, the reality of doing so was very different from anything he'd imagined.

It was different from anything I'd imagined, too. Yes, I'd worried about A.J., especially with his sensitive nature, going off to war—to kill other people. But I'd somehow convinced myself that, with all his rigorous training, it would be...what? Easy for him? Well, maybe not easy, but not agonizing. I guessed I had thought it would be just part of the job. Part of being in a war.

War. The ugliest word in any language.

I was still standing with my hand on the phone receiver when Randy rolled into the kitchen in his wheelchair.

"What's wrong?" he asked. "Who was on the phone?"

"A.J.," I replied, then told him all about the call. "He's grief-stricken–like he might as well have killed his best friend. We were cut off before I got much of a chance to say anything to him. Not that I knew what on Earth to say that would make him feel any better. I told him to talk to the chaplain again, but I'm worried he won't do it, that he'll just torture himself in silence over this."

Randy looked at me blankly for a few moments. Then, with a sigh and a half-shrug–he still couldn't get his left shoulder to lift into a proper, two-shouldered shrug– he just turned his wheelchair around and the left the room.

I stared at the empty doorway, stunned at his lack of response–and yet not really surprised. His lack of compassion, lack of *any* emotion, had become par for the course. I just wasn't yet used to it. I still expected him to be the man I'd married.

He wasn't, though, and I suddenly realized that he was unlikely ever to be that man again. At that moment, it finally sank in that the stroke had affected Randy's brain far more than the doctors had told us–or, perhaps, even knew. Or maybe they had told me, and I simply hadn't wanted to believe it. I hadn't wanted to accept that my husband, once a vibrant, strong-minded, engaging man, was gone for good. The husk of a man who remained was capable of little more than sitting in a wheelchair and waiting–for a miracle or death. I wasn't at all sure that he cared even slightly which might come first.

On top of the troubling call from A.J., I just couldn't cope with such a disturbing insight about my husband. I felt overwhelmed and besieged from all sides. I wanted to run away, to leave my life and all its insolvable problems behind and just go somewhere else. Anywhere but here.

I ran as far as the burning barrel, which had become my place to vent my frustrations. Marcie followed me, but when I started screaming and sobbing, she got scared and ran back to the house. I didn't mind. I wanted to be alone.

Yet being alone meant feeling more than ever the hollow emptiness inside me. I hated it. It was worse than helplessness, worse even than feeling as if I was the only person left in the world.

I cried and shouted until I was hoarse. Then I went back to the house and started making dinner. What else was there to do?

Later that evening, I told Darin about A.J.'s phone call. He seemed to understand immediately how A.J. was feeling. He said that he himself could never be a Marine because he could never kill anyone. He felt sorry for his brother and didn't know what he would have said to console him, any more than I had known what to say.

Then Darin did a beautiful thing. He took my hands in his and said, "Let's pray for him together, Mom. You always said that Jesus listens closer when people pray together. Right?"

I am so blessed to have such incredible children. We prayed together for A.J., doing our best to send a lightning bolt up to Heaven on his behalf.

It was hard to sleep that night. I tossed and turned, then finally got up and made some herb tea. I had three cups.

Afterward, I managed to fall asleep. I was still aware enough, though, to know that I was dreaming. It was a story I had recently read; but this time I was in it, and it felt real.

I was carrying a large cross across my shoulders. I looked up and saw that I was standing in front of a large door–so large that it dwarfed me, as if I had fallen into the Jack and the Beanstalk fairytale. I felt a Presence and knew it was the Lord. I was delighted, because He was just who I was wanting to talk to.

"Greetings, Jo Anne. Are you troubled?" He asked me.

He knew I was, but I answered anyway. "Yes, Lord. I can't carry the cross you've given me anymore. It's grown too heavy–or I've grown too weak. I need You to help me."

"My child, if you cannot bear the weight of your cross, simply place it in the room you'll find beyond this door and choose a different one. You'll find other crosses inside. Pick any one you wish. But you cannot leave empty-handed."

I was so relieved, the instant the Lord opened the large door for me, I hurried inside as fast as I could manage and dropped the heavy cross I was carrying in a corner. Then, preparing to choose another, much smaller one, I looked around.

My eyes widened in shock at what I saw. So many crosses! And they were all *huge*. Some standing upright even touched the ceiling of the enormous room. I walked slowly around the room, examining every nook and cranny, searching for a cross I thought I could manage. There didn't seem to be one. Then, finally, I found it: tiny cross lying flat on the floor in the darkest corner of the room.

Pointing to it, I told the Lord, "I'll take that one."

The Lord smiled. "Jo Anne, that is the cross you just brought in."

My Son is a Marine

FIVE

The best therapy, in my opinion, is laughter. I knew the best thing I could do for A.J. would be to try to make him laugh. So I sat down and wrote him this letter:

Dear A.J.,

I just got off the phone with you. It was heartbreaking to hear the overwhelming sadness in your voice. Remember what I always told you about the bad times in our lives? It consists of four simple words: This too shall pass. I want you to do me a big favor. I want you to read this letter, then close your eyes and think about the times in our lives I'm going to describe. They are forever engraved on my heart. I laugh every time I think about them. I hope they'll make you laugh, too, although I know you don't feel like laughing right now.

So here goes....

It was 1992, and you were eight years old. I was a sales rep for a company that distributed paper goods. My days were long, and the last thing I wanted to do when I got home was talk to telemarketers. Caller ID didn't yet exist–at least, not in our household–so we always answered the phone.

One particular day, we had five calls in a row from telemarketers–everything from aluminum-siding salesmen to somebody informing us that we had qualified as the grand prizewinner in a sweepstakes contest. I'd had enough of it and was ready to rip the phone out of the wall, and you offered to help me screen the next call.

Sure enough, the phone rang again. I prompted you to answer it and if it were another sales pitch, we would get rid of the person together.

"Hello?" you said into the receiver.

There was a pause. Then you very politely asked, "May I ask who's calling please?"

Another pause.

I watched as your eyes widened and your mouth gaped open. "Yes, ma'am!" you gasped, "I'll tell her. Hold on! I'll tell her right now!"

You put the phone against your chest and looked at me with terror written all over your face. "Mom!" you said, your voice shaking. "It's the F.B.I.! Swear to God! The lady is from the F.B.I.! She says she wants to talk to you!"

Unconvinced–what in the world would the F.B.I. want with me?–I took the phone from you. "Hello?" I said in my best "who exactly are you?" tone.

"Is this Jo Anne Allen?" a woman asked sternly.

"Yes," I answered, anxiously awaiting her next words.

"Mrs. Allen, this is Sandra from B.F.I. Waste Management. We understand your trash service is currently with…"

That's all I heard. I couldn't even let her finish her sentence before I started laughing hysterically. I don't know how long it was before I could catch my breath and stop laughing long enough to explain to the poor woman.

I still laugh every time I think about that story.

Then there's this one–my all-time favorite:

You were always a curious child. When I told you not to touch something, you did it anyway, not because you were bad, but because you simply couldn't help yourself.

Once, just before Darin was born, you were watching me use a hot iron to curl my hair. I set it on the bathroom counter and told you sternly, "Don't touch that, A.J. It's hot."

I continued putting on my makeup, and a few minutes later, I saw you in the mirror reaching for the curling iron.

"No!" I yelled.

It was too late. You touched it and, of course, got burned. The curling iron left a big red spot on your finger that lasted a week or two. But once it healed, I thought you had forgotten all about it.

Then, just a few weeks later, I had Darin. The doctor used forceps to pull him out, leaving marks all over his head. Even when he was just six weeks old, he still had bald spots where the forceps had been. The spots were bright red, and you asked me about them several times. It was difficult to explain to you, since you were so young, but I did my best.

One day, you went with Darin and me to the grocery store, with Darin sitting in his car seat, inside the cart. We reached the checkout counter, and several elderly ladies were in line ahead of us. They oohed and ahhed at my tiny bundle of joy, until one woman started talking to you—thinking, I guess, that you must be feeling left out. She began asking you questions about the baby.

"Is that your baby brother or baby sister?" she asked.

You beamed. "That's my baby brother!"

"What happened to his head?" she asked you, looking at the red forceps marks.

With no hesitation whatsoever, you said, "Mommy burned him with the curling iron!"

The looks on those old ladies' faces were priceless.

"A.J.!" I exclaimed. "I did not!"

You put your hands on your hips and said, "Did, too!"

I never went back into that store again.

I hope being reminded of these special times lightens your heart at least a little bit.

Now, I want to tell you a secret. Please don't tell anyone–especially Dad! When he's asleep–really, deeply asleep...and I can tell when he is by his snoring–I sit on the bed by him and lay my hands on his left side. I gently move them up and down from his head to his toes, and while I'm doing that, I pray that all the functions go back to being perfect.

I know you'll think it's crazy, but it can't do him any harm, so...well, why not? I usually spend about fifteen minutes a night asking God to make him whole again. You know that God likes people to pester Him about things. That way, He knows we are diligently seeking Him. I think I must be God's number-one pest!

Your dog has a new name. "Mercy Marcie." She found a nest of baby rabbits. She doesn't try to hurt them. Even though she's been neutered, she still has her motherly instincts. She just lies with them and licks them. The mama must have been some coyote's dinner because these little ones were sure hungry. Needless to say, I've been bottle-feeding all seven of them!

Bo has a job pending once he's through with college. He can't wait to make the big bucks! Me, either. I hope he becomes a millionaire! Then he'll be able to take care of me!

You know that prayer thing I do every night for Dad? I have another secret. I do the same for you. Except I have to use the picture of you that I carry around in my head. I sit on your bed and hold your pillow against me the way I use to hold you went you were little. Then I pray for your safety and for complete healing from whatever troubles you. I always pray for you, A.J. Remember that.

Love you way past all the constellations!
Mom

A.J. called home a few more times over the following month. He was quiet, but eager to talk to us. We didn't speak about the war or what he had been doing. Instead, I spent those precious few minutes making him laugh. I told him jokes and talked about things that Marcie had done. I made him eager to get back to us. I promised homemade peach pie and ice cream, lasagna made with Velveeta cheese, and an endless supply of soft peanut butter cookies.

Then, toward the end of July, we got the first piece of good news, via the telephone, that we'd had in a long time:

"Hello? A.J.?" I always knew his calls by the strange area code that showed up on the Caller ID.

"Hey!" came the delayed response.

"How's my favorite Marine?"

"That depends on you. What's your schedule like on August second?"

I looked at the calendar hanging beside the phone. "It's open. Why?"

"I need you to pick me up at the airport."

"Whoo-hoo!" I yelled.

"I'm bringing Dunning home with me. Is that okay?"

"Of course it's okay! Tell him we'd love to have him. But doesn't his family want to see him?"

"Mom, don't say anything about this, but he had it pretty rough growing up. Neither of his parents really wanted custody of him. He's a real neat guy, too. They'd feel different if they could see what a great Marine he is. We get a week's leave before we have to go back to Camp LeJeune, and he has no place to go."

"He does now," I said. "You know I'll make sure he feels welcome. What time does your plane get in?"

"That's where we have a slight problem. We can't get a flight into Little Rock that day. Can you pick us up in Memphis? There's a flight that gets in at 8:00 p.m. on August second."

"No problem." Memphis was a five-hour drive from our farm, and I relished the thought of having all that time to spend with A.J. "I'll be there, eight o'clock sharp! Do you remember what I look like? I have highlighted blond hair, I'm short, and I–"

"Mom!" A.J. exclaimed in that happy tone I hadn't heard from him in months. "I could *never* forget what you look like! I'm the one you might not recognize."

"Why is that?" I asked.

"I just look different. I think my nose got bigger."

I had to laugh.

"No, really," he said. "I thought I was through growing, but I guess my face is trying to catch up to my body. People always tell me I have a big nose, and one guy started calling me Pinocchio."

I continued to laugh. "Is that all? People used to call me *thunder thighs* in high school."

The sound of A.J.'s laughter came through loud and clear–the first true, uninhibited laughter I had heard from him in ages. I couldn't wait to see him.

Naturally, I got to the airport three hours early, which didn't make A.J.'s flight arrive any faster. It did, however, cost me a pretty penny. I think they must sell more Elvis souvenirs at Memphis International than they do at Graceland. It was only August, but I had my Christmas shopping finished in the first sixty minutes of my three-hour wait.

It seemed crowded at this airport. Besides all the normal stores and various restaurants, something unusual caught my eye. A young woman, appearing to be in her mid twenties, had an apple cart set up next to the busy walkway. Watching her tend her apples, it was quite obvious she was blind.

She seemed happy and congenial as she conversed with her customers. I decided I had to buy some apples.

"Are these red delicious?" I asked approaching her cart.

"Oh, hi," she responded and then smiled. "I've been told they are. I don't know colors so I can't tell you for sure."

"Red delicious is the name of a brand," I said. "These look like them. Bright red and beyond yummy."

"They're 85 cents each. How many would you like?" she asked.

What a charming little saleswoman, I thought as I looked for the biggest ones displayed.

"I'll need three," I said thinking of my two new passengers.

"That will be $2.55."

"Fair enough," I said and handed her a five-dollar bill. I was amazed that she knew what amount of currency I gave her. She reached in her change box and withdrew $2.45, and then counted the change back to me.

"I'm impressed, young lady!" I said.

"Thank you," she replied. "They taught us at the blind school all about currency and things like that. I've never had to give someone change back for a hundred dollar bill yet."

I laughed. "What exactly do those look like?"

She was amused. "I can tell you what they *feel* like."

I learned her name was Charann. She was blind from birth. Her parents owned an apple orchard. I told her about A.J. and Wendall and how they were both Marines just coming home from Iraq.

"Marines? Wow! Can I meet them? I've never met anyone who was over there. I'd like to...to thank them for defending our country and giving me my freedom to sell apples. Would you introduce me to them when they get here?" she asked.

I carefully studied her as she spoke to me. I was amazed at her words and felt totally blessed that I was able to spend a little time getting to know her.

Although she couldn't see them, her eyes were a beautiful shade of green. She was about 5'5" and a little on the pudgy side. She wore a tucked in white shirt with black slacks and flat shoes. Her creamy complexion was plain. Her best feature was her coal black hair, which she wore in a ponytail.

I promised her I would return with my two Marines and left.

By the time they finally announced the arrival of A.J.'s flight–thirty minutes late–I was a nervous wreck. Shaking with excitement, I watched the passengers disembark. There were a number of soldiers, and they must have thought I was crazy for examining them as closely as I did. A.J. had painted a picture of himself as a whole different person. I couldn't believe that I'd really fail to recognize my own son, but....

"Tell me a story!"

That voice, I definitely knew.

"Oh, my God!" I screamed, and half a second later, I was being picked up off the floor and swung around by a pair of strong arms. I hadn't even seen him coming down the ramp.

"Set me down," I ordered. "I want to look at you." Although, I didn't know how much I'd be able to see through the tears pouring down my cheeks.

Still, as he stood grinning before me, I realized that something about him *was* different. He'd been right. His nose was bigger. As I tilted his head to the side so I could see it better, a voice came from behind A.J.

"He broke it."

"Mom, this is Dunning," A.J. said as he grabbed his friend's arm and pulled him around. "Dunning, this is my mom. Everyone calls her Jo Anne."

"Actually, you can call me Mom," I said.

"That'd be cool! Would you mind...Mom?" Dunning asked softly.

I looked at that child of God and wondered how any parent could have rejected him. He'd have been a towhead if his hair were grown out. He had a few pimples but not many, and a few crooked teeth that only gave him character. He was small in stature, but looked tough as nails, yet he had a boyish charm that reminded me of Opie on the *Andy Griffith Show*. His hazel eyes shone with a light that Christians recognize. I liked him immediately.

"I can't call you Dunning," I said. "What's your first name, son?"

His gaze fell to his boots as he replied. "Wendall."

"Wendall Dunning," I said. "Now that's a name you can trust."

Wendall beamed.

I pulled both him and A.J. into a hug and just stood there, embracing them, for a good five minutes. It seemed as if the tears would never stop flowing.

Finally, A.J. said, "Mom...how about if we pick this up at home? I'd kinda like to get out of here."

"Sure," I replied, pulling back and giving them both a watery smile. "Let's get your bags."

A.J. shook his head and gave his duffle a slap. "We're set. We've only got our carry-ons. Let's go home."

Then I remembered Charann. "Hey! You two need to come with me first. I bought these apples from a sweet young blind girl right over there. She asked that I introduce you to her. Can you spare a minute?"

"Sure!" they said in unison.

"Charann?" I asked as we approached her. "I brought my son and his friend here to meet you. This is A.J., and this is Wendall."

I took their hands to touch hers. She reached over and gave each Marine a hug from her heart and then whispered to each one separately, "Thank you for what you are doing. It makes me proud."

You could have heard a pin drop. No one else had said those words to these young men. Here she was, blind and unable to see their expression. I wished she could have because it would have melted her heart. They were overwhelmed.

I thought how unbelievable the moment was. She was blind, yet she could see better than anyone else. What a gift she gave to A.J., Wendall, and me.

My Son is a Marine

Six

Once we were on the road, I quickly discovered what a good thing it was that Wendall was with us. He encouraged A.J. to talk openly about their experiences, stressing that it was good therapy. I knew how hard it was to pry anything out of my son when he didn't want to let go of it, but Wendall was persistent.

"We have to get it out!" he kept saying. "We weren't allowed to talk about what was going on while it was happening, but now it's over! For us, anyway. We can't get into trouble for telling your mom. Anyway, I need to talk about it, and I know you do, too. It was messed up."

"The whole war thing was bad," A.J. agreed. Then, after a long pause, he added, "I guess we can discuss it a little."

At that, my opinion of Wendall rose several notches.

"But after this," A.J. warned, "I never want to talk about it again."

"I'd just like to hear it once," I said. "We have plenty of time–five hours before we get home. I've thought about you constantly–all of you–and I'd really like to hear what's happened to you over there."

They started from the beginning, when they were in Kuwait.

"None of us knew what to expect," A.J. said. "We knew those from our own platoon, but more troops kept coming and coming. We knew a war was about to start. We built so many bridges–like over the Tigris and

Euphrates rivers–it was hard to keep up with the actual number. The weather was tolerable then, a little cool, but wearing all the gear kept us plenty warm. And the work kept us hungry.

"Trouble was," Wendall put in, "the Marines didn't plan the food right. We ate C rations, which we figured out real quick stood for *crap*. They're called MREs–meals ready to eat. We all swore they had to be from the '70s, they were so freaking old! But we were so hungry, it didn't matter.

"It mattered a lot more that there wasn't enough to go around," muttered A.J. "We got one meal a day, and we had to make it last, like they taught us in boot camp. We knew to eat our crackers for breakfast, the main dish for lunch, and the pound cake for supper. We all lost weight, but we had some energy. Eventually, more food was shipped in, and we had two meals a day. That was a lot better.

"Did you have any free time at all?" I asked.

"Yeah," A.J. replied. "That's when we all got to know one another. We knew something big was about to hit, and we talked about it a lot. We were told there would be casualties, and we talked about dying and how we felt about it."

Behind me, in the backseat, Wendall gave a short, ironic laugh. "Each of us knew, in our own hearts, that it wouldn't be us. We'd be the one that made it home safe."

"We talked about our families," A.J. continued. "We got to know each other's sisters and brothers' names and favorite things and even our deepest secrets–figured we might as well share those, too. Maybe just in case it turned out we *did* end up in on the casualty list."

"Tell me about the other Marines in your group," I said.

Going back and forth, A.J. and Wendall filled me in on the others. There was Happenstahl, a giant of a guy, older than the rest and a self-admitted "screw-up" who was always getting into trouble with the law; he knew he'd land in jail sooner or later, so he'd joined the Marines. Then there was Harrison, a redhead from Tennessee, funny, good-looking, and a typical playboy whose secret wish was to have a harem. Logan, leader of a black street gang in L.A., had been smart enough to realize he needed to get off the streets before he wound up dead; he'd had trouble learning to take orders in boot camp, but he was turning out to be a great Marine.

Going down the roster, A.J. added, "Gurule's the Mexican in the group. She's tough and–"

"Wait!" I interrupted. "Gurule is female?"

"Yeah, she's been a female her entire life."

"You don't need to get smart about it," I said. "Is she pretty?"

"Mom, she's a *Marine*. We don't even notice that she's a girl."

"A.J. I realize she's a Marine, but I can't help but wonder about her. I'm picturing a petite little thing among all you Arnold Schwarzenegger wannabes."

"*Petite?* Mom, her nickname is Gorilla. She's incredible. She knows how to fight, how to kill, and how to survive."

"The only female, though...you'd think..."

"Mom, not even Harrison, Mr. Concubine himself, hits on her. She outweighs us all by at least thirty pounds! We don't even know her first name. She's just

Gurule. End of story."

I shut up and listened as A.J. continued.

"You met Mason and know all about him. You know Dunning now, since he's your new adopted son, and that leaves me."

"What's your deep dark secret?" I teased.

"He doesn't have any," came Wendall's reply from the backseat. "At least, he doesn't have *dark* secrets. He just has deep ones. He *knows* things. And he's got more peace of mind than any of the rest of us."

I looked at Wendall's eyes in my rearview mirror. They were full of sincerity. Then I glanced at A.J., who was looking embarrassed by his friend's words.

Wendall continued. "We had a lot of time on our hands. We talked about God and how He fit into the whole picture. Like, who's side is He on since He loves everyone, right? Then A.J. started telling us all these stories–ones you told him when he was a little kid. And, somehow, things started to make sense. I mean, we had to rely on *something* besides ourselves. So why not go for the gold? Why not rely on something so powerful that nothing can overcome it, not even death? The only thing that powerful is God. It took several weeks for it to sink in, but all of us eventually got there. A.J. suggested we pray for our safety–together, not as seven individuals. So we did. He led us at first, then encouraged us to take turns. We knew there were a lot of other people praying for us because of the letters from you and others, and we got to feeling like God had put a shield around us."

"That's wonderful," I said. "And amazing that you *all* came to the Lord in such a short time, and so strongly."

"Well, we had a good teacher," Wendall said, giving

A.J., who was studiously ignoring him, a punch on the shoulder. "Your son isn't ashamed to talk about his faith. We weren't too cooperative at first, but you know how God works. The *idea* of Him starts in your head, then makes its way down to your heart, where it becomes faith. Like A.J. told us, we're like seeds that a farmer planted. Some make it. Some don't. We just all happened to make it."

And seeds nurtured and tended properly had a lot better chance of making it than the ones left to fend for themselves. Pride in my son's abilities as "gardener" swelled inside me.

"Okay, that's enough," A.J. said. "Let's dwell on something else."

"Sure," Wendall agreed–too easily, I thought. I saw him help himself to another peanut butter cookie from the tin sitting beside him. Then he lounged back in the seat, took a bite, and said, "Let's tell Mom the puppy story."

"No!" A.J. almost yelled. "I hate that memory!"

"Too bad. I need to tell it. So, Mom, it was like this. It was April second, and we were all sitting in this truck. It was too hot for all our clothes and backpacks, especially scrunched in together like we were, all twenty or more of us, in that open flatbed.

"We should have been moving, but the convoy we were in had come to a dead stop. There were too many vehicles ahead of us for us to be able to see what the hold up was, so we just sat there and waited and drank our water. We didn't talk much. We'd been there maybe an hour when one guy pointed up the hill beside our truck and said, 'Hey! Check out that puppy.'

"And sure enough, it was just a little guy, just about

old enough to get weaned. It was whimpering and looking around. We all watched for a couple minutes. Then Mason jumped out of the truck. We yelled at him to get back in. He said he felt sorry for the pup. It was hot outside, and he could give it some water at least. He took his canteen.

"Then the sergeant jumped out, tackled him, and said something we couldn't hear. They both came back to the rig. We wanted to know what the deal was. Mason was just doing what we were all thinking about doing. "'It's a trap,' Sarge said. 'The first one who goes over there and rescues that dog gets us all blown up. Get it?'"

"So then we understood. The Iraqis have this thing with bombs and using our weaknesses against us. Most Americans love animals. Why not tug at the ol' heartstrings? Why not put a helpless little puppy out on a hill with no food or water? See how long before some gullible Marine will take before he runs to it to save its life. They're watching from somewhere, and they wait. When the pup gets picked up, they detonate the bomb, and we die."

I felt the heat of anger rising inside me at Wendall's matter-of-fact explanation. Using an innocent puppy as bait! Playing on an enemy's morality–their very *humanity*! How evil! But then, war was evil, wasn't it? As Wendall had said at the start, it was "messed up."

Wendall continued. "A.J. was having more of a problem with that puppy sitting there and doing nothing for it than the rest of us. Not that we weren't all bothered, but he'd gotten your letter about Marcie getting bitten by that cottonmouth. So he was worried about her, and there was that puppy on the hill, and...well, he got real quiet.

"So the minutes turned into an hour, and we were all watching this pup. It whimpered a lot at first, but then it gave up. It just laid down and squirmed some every now and then. It was pretty close, so we could all see it. Except A.J. He said his eyes were bad, and he only saw something fluffy. Just as well he couldn't see its face. We all watched it die."

There was a moment of silence, then Wendall said, "Ready for the God thing?"

I blinked. "The God thing?" I couldn't get the image of that helpless canine out of my mind.

"Yeah," Wendall said. "A.J. said he prayed for Marcie the entire time we sat there. He asked God to save her if we couldn't save that pup. Could He just do this one thing for him? I never witnessed such concentrated praying in my life. A.J. was begging God."

"When, exactly, did this happen again?" I asked, my heart quickening.

"April second, at 1600 hours, ma'am," Wendall said. "He got your letter about Marcie that morning. Then we had to head out on the convoy."

"April second was when I went to the vet to get Marcie. They'd taken her off life support the night before, and the vet said she wouldn't make it through the night. I got there around seven in the morning, expecting to pick up her body."

"And we were nine hours ahead–1600, or four p.m., as you civilians say," Wendall grinned. "A God thing, wouldn't ya say?"

I couldn't say anything. I could only nod in agreement, as I looked at A.J. My expression was one of utter amazement.

A.J. swallowed and clearly felt uncomfortable. "Speaking of Marcie...how is she, anyway?"

"She's waiting for you, stubby tail and all," I said with a smile. "Expect to romp with her for at least an hour."

A.J. smiled. Of course, he would oblige.

"Your turn, A.J. Tell her about the first night," Wendall said.

A.J. took a deep breath. "The first night the war was announced had to be the worst. There were scuds–huge missiles–fired every five to fifteen minutes. If any of us got an hour of sleep that night, I'd be surprised. I sure didn't. It was way too close for comfort. The war was in Iraq, but the scuds actually made it to Kuwait. They would have caused major damage if they'd hit, but we were pretty good at intercepting them. We didn't get them all, and the ones that did hit...well, they caused a lot of damage. But no one we knew was killed.

"This went on for a week. It was constant chaos. Two of us shared a fighting hole. We would take turns sleeping. It was so intense. A month passed and seemed like eternity. The weather was unreal. Temperatures soared well over 130 degrees. I don't see how anything could survive that kind of heat. The thing that saved us was the lack of humidity. Can you imagine that heat with humidity added in? It was as if we were all in hell! Which is really how we felt.

"We could see that nothing plant-wise really survived in that part of the world. Kuwait has no grass, trees, or shrubs to speak of. Walking through the sand was like wading through four feet of water. It was work to get anywhere. We would hold off urinating for hours because we couldn't stand the walk to the latrine.

"The sand blew constantly in our faces. There was never any relief from the heat to get any rest or to feel clean even after we sponged off. We never saw a single cloud the entire time we were there. Honestly, how do people live there?

"During that month, we couldn't take a shower. We had no facilities. We used baby wipes to sponge ourselves, but they never really made us feel clean. Just less gritty. That sand was merciless! It dug itself into every single fold of skin! My ears and nostrils were caked with that crap. I knew everyone had to feel as filthy as I did. We were miserable wearing our dirty clothes. When we changed underwear or socks, we just threw the ones we had on out. As if we could go to the local Laundromat and wash them!

"And then the care packages started coming. It was always the highlight of the day. We were so hungry for American food. We got beef jerky, candy, and homemade cookies, but you already know that. They were great for snacking and definitely better than the runny cheese in the C rations. The Kool-Aid was a favorite. Our only drink was water, so we were grateful for anything to perk it up.

"We shared everything. It was so great when those packages and letters started arriving. They came from elementary school kids and from old folks in nursing homes. Just everywhere–and from total strangers. It was nice to know how much people cared. I still have all my letters. I used the gallon plastic bags you sent me to keep them in. I didn't want a single one to get wrecked. I plan to keep them forever–kind of like your shoebox, Mom.

These will all go into *my* shoebox. I have 216 of them."

"I have all mine, too," Wendall added.

They both fell silent for a minute or two. Then Wendall piped up, "We got to go to Baghdad once. What a trip! It looks just like on TV, except we saw the weapons stockpiled there. The Marines got to blow them up. We dug holes and stuck them all in and covered them up. Then we lit one and backed off. Sometimes we'd shoot at the pile, and they'd all go off. It was crazy.

"You know the bizarre thing? Going through Baghdad, we noticed that people's backyards were all cluttered with debris from the bombs. Guess those poor people lived in fear all their lives. Maybe now they won't have to. But most of their houses were wrecked, everything they owned gone. Their male kids were forced to fight, even the real young ones. I saw some that looked like they were just fifteen years old. They would jump on the soldiers with knives. They had to be shot because–"

"Stop," A.J. exclaimed. "Don't talk about that."

Wendall met my gaze in the rearview mirror. Then, directing his attention to the back of A.J.'s head, he said, "Okay, then *you* talk. We agreed we'd talk about everything one time, then never repeat it again. You can't keep things like this bottled up forever. It does something to your head."

"You want me to get stuff out?" A.J. retorted. "Fine. Okay. I will." Then, to me, he said, "We had several incidents when young Iraqi men approached us. We had to be on guard. There were a lot of suicide bombings, so we couldn't trust them, even if they were smiling. We had to grab our guns and get into firing position, ready for anything.

"Sometimes, though, your gut tells you when it's dangerous. A couple times I felt totally at ease when they approached. Three of them stopped and reached into their pockets for something. They took out paper money that had Saddam's picture on it. Then they spit on the picture, threw the money on the ground next to our feet, and said *'Saddam!'* as if it was a curse word."

"A.J.," Wendall began, "that isn't–"

"You wanted me to talk. I'm talking. I'm going to tell Mom about my camel ride. Iraq is full of wild camels that travel in herds. We saw them everywhere. They're social creatures, like deer. All the camels just had one hump. The only thing I didn't like about my camel ride was the stupid man who owned it. You know how I hate people being mean to animals. This jerk wouldn't stop hitting it with a stick. I told him to back off, but he didn't get it."

"I've heard camels can be very ornery," I said. "But you're right. That's no excuse for beating an animal."

"Mom?" Wendall said, then winked when I glanced at him in the rearview.

I laughed. "Yes, Son?"

"Get A.J. to tell you how he broke his nose."

A.J. squirmed in his seat. "Dunning..."

Wendall continued. "He saved my life. Our truck flipped over when we were attacked, and we were all stuck inside, except A.J. He'd been driving, and he was thrown clear when we flipped. He got me out–and broke his nose doing it. Then he and I got the others out. Then the truck exploded."

My hands clenched the steering wheel. I gave A.J. a sideways glance and found him staring out the side window, avoiding my gaze.

"Uh...Mom?" Wendall continued. "Get him to tell you the *whole* story. He won't talk about it at all, but I think he needs to. He needs to relive it at least once. Then he can draw a line in the sand and start over."

It took several minutes of persuading before A.J. would agree.

"A'right, a'right," he said, then, in warning tones, added, "But I'm only going to say it once. I want your word, Mom, that you'll never make me talk about it again, after this. I'm trying to forget it ever happened."

"Swear on the Holy Bible," I said. "I will never make you talk about it again." *But I might talk about it,* I added silently, *just not to you.*

"Okay," he began. "We were headed out to repair a bridge that had been blown up by the Iraqis. We were all grumbling because we'd just built it, and already it was destroyed. Well, most of it was. We were going to see what was salvageable and what would have to be rebuilt.

"We were about three hours into the drive. Sarge was tired, so he let me do the driving. It was Dunning and me, Sarge, Happenstahl, Logan, Gurule, Mason, and Harrison.

"The mission was totally uneventful until a group of about thirty Iraqis–kids, all of them, maybe between twelve and eighteen–came bolting out of nowhere and threw a grenade at us. It hit the truck. It flipped over, and suddenly there was sand everywhere. Like Dunning said, I was thrown clear, but everyone else was stuck inside the truck, which was upside down. The attackers were just watching, because the gas line was leaking, and they knew it would explode.

"I...well, I panicked, I think. It felt like I was totally

out of my body again. Except it wasn't anything like the experience I had when I was three. I wasn't floating serenely in the clouds this time, and there weren't any angels in sight. But I felt God's presence, and that's all that mattered. It's like I was watching myself. I knew I didn't have much time, because I could smell the leaking gas line.

"They were all screaming inside the truck. I jumped up on the tire to the passenger side, and tried to open the door, but it wouldn't budge. I begged God to help me, and finally I got it opened. Dunning was right there, and I pulled him out, and he started helping me. Happenstahl was the hardest to get out because he's so big, and he was crammed into the back. Sarge lifted Harrison, Gurule, and Logan to me and Dunning, then he climbed out himself. Then, while he was grabbing for the rifles and the radio and calling in for help, Dunning and I got Mason, who was unconscious on the floor in the front seat. Then we all ran as fast as we could, with Gurule and Logan helping Harrison, who had a broken leg. We got about fifty feet from the truck before she blew."

By this time in A.J.'s recitation, my knuckles were white around the wheel. I shuddered, thinking about how close my son had come to being killed.

"We hit the deck, and for about half a minute, just stayed there. Mason was still out cold, and we realized that, besides Harrison's broken leg, Logan had split open his shoulder, and Dunning got...well..."

"Go ahead. Say it," Wendall prompted. "I got knocked hard in the crotch. Made me puke. And my stomach hurt for days. Still does sometimes. But the doc can't find anything wrong. And" –he snatched another cookie from the tin beside him– "I can still down these peanut butter cookies just fine, so whatever it is, can't be too bad." He shot me a grin in the mirror, then waved a hand at A.J. "Continue."

"So..." A.J. went on, "We were more or less in shock. But there were still the Iraqis who'd thrown the grenade. With all the smoke and fire from the truck, we'd lost sight of them. But they hadn't left. Out of nowhere, they started attacking us. Before we could even get up, Happenstahl got stabbed twice. He was screaming and bleeding all over the place. Sarge yelled for us to take our positions, that the Iraqis might have more grenades or even bombs and that we should start shooting. Only he and Gurule and I had our rifles. And there were twenty or thirty Iraqis. Most of them were wearing street clothes, and the only weapons they had were knives. But we didn't realize that then."

A.J. paused for a couple of seconds. Then, taking a deep breath, he continued. "I was standing in front of Happenstahl, protecting him, and one of the Iraqis came running toward me. I let him get about five feet away. Then I shot him. He...he looked at me...like he couldn't believe I'd done it. Then he just fell."

Silence hung heavy in the car for a full minute, but I didn't attempt to interrupt. Nor did Wendall. Finally, A.J. heaved another deep breath and continued.

"Then this other Iraqi came running over to the guy I'd shot and flung himself down beside him. He was screaming and crying, and I realized they must be friends. Maybe brothers. Meanwhile, Sarge shot a bunch, and so did Gurule, and the ones left started running away. They disappeared as fast as they'd appeared. Later, we counted nine dead. But the one who'd stayed back with his friend didn't even try to get away. He kept holding the...the dead guy in his arms and crying and saying stuff nobody understood. But it was pretty plain what he meant."

I said carefully, "Love and grief are universal, A.J. They transcend any language barrier. They're part of what makes us human."

"Yeah," he agreed quietly. Then, on a ragged sigh, he added, "So, I dropped my gun and went over and squatted down next to the guy who was crying. Then Sarge screams something at me about his having a knife, but I didn't really hear it. I looked at the dead kid. Then I looked at his friend–or brother...Mama, I saw how sad he was. And he held his arms out to show me he didn't have any weapons. And I reached down and picked up the dead kid, and I held him and...and I asked God to forgive me, because it hurt so bad. But how can God forgive me when I can't forgive myself? I must have stared at his face for an entire minute before Sarge grabbed my arm and pulled me off.

"'Back off!' he yelled at me. 'This is the enemy! Happenstahl, Harrison, and Logan are injured, we lost our truck, we're sitting out here like a bunch of ducks on water, and you're feeling guilty? Get over there and help the others. Count how many canteens we have. There might not be enough to last until help gets here. We're three hours from the base.' Then he ordered Gurule to keep watch on the hill where the Iraqis had disappeared and to be ready to shoot."

A.J. paused before going on. I didn't say a word. I didn't look into his eyes as he was recalling every horrific detail. I kept my eyes on the road and let him finish.

"The one uninjured Iraqi wouldn't leave his friend. I wouldn't have either. We took him prisoner. We gathered up the nine bodies and were told we would bury them when the other truck arrived with supplies. They would have shovels and water. We would continue our mission tomorrow."

A.J. stopped, and, after a minute, when he didn't pick up the story again, Wendall unbuckled his seat belt and sat close behind my seat. "Let me finish."

I looked at A.J. and noticed his eyes were filled with tears. I couldn't bring myself to push it.

"It had been almost three hours," Wendall said, "and the Iraqi was dripping with sweat. We all knew he had to be thirsty. He sat with his friend in his lap and waited. It was like he wanted to be buried with him. We wondered if the others would return, but we figured they realized we'd shoot them the instant their heads popped over the hill.

"A.J. couldn't stop looking at the two Iraqi kids. We told him it was part of war–that the kid had been trying to jump him. We told him to look at Happenstahl, who was still bleeding through the compresses we had on his leg and arm. Mason came to and showed everyone the knot on his head. It was as big as a baseball. He kept asking everyone for Excedrin, but of course the medicine was in the truck, which wasn't a truck anymore. Gurule took pictures of it all. She had a camera in her pocket. Everyone was quiet, just waiting for rescue to get there.

"Then A.J. got up and went to the Iraqi soldier. He shook his canteen, which still had some water in it. We had enough, and Sarge had some to spare, too. A.J. offered the water to the Iraqi. The kid looked surprised, but he took the canteen. He swallowed the water in gulps so loud, we could all hear. He was so thirsty. When he'd finished the whole canteen, he gave it back, empty, to A.J.

"And then something really weird happened. A.J. hugged him. He said, 'I'm sorry, man.' The Iraqi seemed pretty overwhelmed over that little gesture and held him at arm's length. Then he touched A.J.'s nose and showed him the blood on his finger. Then A.J. touched it, too, and looked at the blood on his own finger. He hadn't realized his nose had been broken.

"'Hey! My nose is broken, isn't it?' he said to us. We all told him it was a definite improvement."

I cast a sideways glance at A.J. and saw the corner of his mouth twitching in what might have been a smile.

"What about the truck?" I asked.

"The rescue truck *finally* came. We got food and water, then buried the dead Iraqis. The prisoner was really cooperative. He sat hunched over in the backseat the entire trip back. He never said another word."

Wendall paused for a moment, then said, "That's it, Mom. That's the story of how your son's nose got broken."

"It's quite a story," I replied–the understatement of the year, I figured. "I appreciate your telling me–*both* of you."

The rest of the ride home was quiet. We talked about their plans for the week and things they wanted to do.

A.J. couldn't wait to see Angela, his girlfriend for the last two years of high school. He'd been telling me for the past year or so that she was the only girl for him and that he would marry her someday. I liked it that he said *someday*. I thought nineteen was too young to tie the knot.

Nearing our home, Wendall wanted to know if we had any critters besides Marcie.

"Oh, sure," I replied. "We have two cats, a dog, a few chickens, two horses, a calf, and a donkey. Do you know much about farm animals?"

"I know *nothing* about anything to do with a farm," Wendall said. "This is going to be an excellent adventure for this city boy! Thank you so much for taking me in. I really appreciate it."

My heart went out to Wendall. He was a Marine fighting the war in Iraq, now on a week's leave. He'd had no place to go, and I was glad A.J. had insisted he spend the time with him. Who knew it would turn out to be another "God thing"?

It was late when we got home. Darin was waiting up, though. And, of course, Marcie went nuts.

"Hey, girl," A.J. exclaimed. "You're pretty!"

"That sure is a white dog. You weren't kidding, Allen," Wendall said as he admired the hyper Jack Russell.

"I'm putting you boys together in one room. There's a rollaway for you, Wendall. It's really comfortable. It's almost two in the morning, but I'm wide-awake. Can I help you unpack?" I asked.

"Just that bag there," A.J. said. "That's the one with all my letters and stuff I didn't want lost."

I unzipped the zipper and saw a framed certificate sporting the USMC emblem on the top third of the paper. "What's this?"

"It's something I thought was really cool," A.J. answered.

It was a memo dated March 3, 2003, signed by Major General J.N. Mattis of the United States Marines. It read:

Demonstrate to the world there is No Better Friend, No Worse Enemy, than a United States Marine.

I think they did.

My Son is a Marine

SEVEN

I got up early the next day, eager to spend it with the family.

Randy would sleep late, and that would give me time to whip up something special for breakfast. I decided on waffles and bacon.

"I drink my coffee black," came a familiar voice.

"Hey! You're up with the chickens. Didn't you have jet lag?" I asked as I stared into the sleepy eyes of Lance Corporal Dunning. I reminded myself that everyone in A.J.'s platoon was now at least a lance corporal.

"I can sleep when I'm dead. A.J. wants to pack a year of fun into this week, and I'm with him! I can help with whatever you were going to make for breakfast. I'm starved," he said with a charming smile.

"You mean that double cheeseburger and large French fries from Wendy's isn't still stuck to your ribs?" I asked and then chuckled. We had stopped in Little Rock the night before for some fast food.

"Not a bit. Are your coffee cups up here?" he asked, then opened the wrong cabinet door.

I showed him around the kitchen, explaining that he wasn't a guest. He was *family*. "Just help yourself to whatever you want, whenever you want it," I told him.

I started the bacon frying and let Wendall whip up the batter for the waffles.

"I can't mess that up, can I?" he asked as he stirred the thick batter.

"A.J. does," I quipped. "Once, he decided that chocolate chips would be a nice addition and added an entire bag. We all thought it was a bit much."

Wendall laughed. "I know he's planning on spending time with Angela. Would you mind if I just hung out here? I'd love to ride that four-wheeler he talks about. I've also never been on a horse–except the merry-go-round at the carnival, and I don't think that counts. I'd like to explore the place a bit, too. It'd be a first for me to walk through an open field and not get hollered at for trespassing."

I admired Wendall. He was courteous, adventurous, and helpful.

"Are all Marines like you? I only personally know three now–you, Mason, and A.J."

"We're a rare breed, *Mom,*" Wendall said with all the seriousness he could muster. "I like saying *mom.* It doesn't bug you?"

"Not a bit. In fact, I'm flattered. I've decided I'm going to keep you."

Wendall blushed. "You know, A.J. thinks the world of you. He loves his dad and brothers, too. But he talks about you all the time. He says you've always spent a lot of time with him–and that you're always up for *anything*."

"Like what?" I asked, curious.

"Oh, like swimming, hiking, camping, fishing, four-wheeling, and horseback riding. But his fondest memories are your stories."

"Really?"

"Yes. Stories about him, his brothers, you, his dad. He especially loved Bible stories. And he liked the way you made them more real by changing your voice for different characters. He also loves that story about the three trees, and the one about the barn and the birds. He told those two to all of us, and I'm sure, someday, he'll pass them on to his kids." Pausing to take a swig of his coffee, Wendall added, "He's the best friend I ever had."

"Thank you for sharing that," I said, tears stinging my eyes.

I turned the bacon and started making the waffles.

"Would you tell me about your childhood, Wendall?" I asked, not knowing many details about him. "Where did you grow up?"

"I lived in a trailer with my mom for a while," he replied. "Then I lived in a camper with my dad. I lived mostly in New Mexico, but some in Kansas. I went from school to school, town to town. My folks never married...well, not each other anyway. I have half-sisters and brothers, but we hardly know each other. My mom got pregnant young. She did the best she could. She didn't even get through high school, so you can imagine the jobs she had.

"Now, my *daddy*! There's a character for you. He had coal-black hair, drank a lot, smoked a lot, and worked a little. That's why he lived in a camper. It was a dump. I hated staying with him, but had to until I got older. He had this thing about my hair being blond. He used to put his cigarettes out on my head and say, 'Now you're an ash blond.'"

Shocked, I looked at Wendall, my heart going out to him. But he wasn't crying or showing any other signs of distress. On the contrary, he seemed very matter-of-fact about something that appalled me.

I finished cooking as he continued to talk.

"I started getting into trouble at school when my mom got married. My step-dad didn't want a ready-made family, so she sent me to my dad. Don't think badly about my mom, though. She was just a kid herself."

"Where is she now?" I asked. "Do you want to call her and tell her you're in the States?"

Wendall refilled his coffee cup and then walked to the kitchen table to sit down.

"I have no clue what her phone number is. I think she still lives in New Mexico. My stepdad was in sales there and did fairly well. They moved to a new house a few years ago. She's got four kids by him now, I think. We lost contact, because she didn't want any problems in her marriage. I managed to get through school, bum around for a year, and then I decided to make something of myself. So I did something crazy."

"You joined the USMC," I said.

"Yep. I picked the branch that was the hardest. I wanted to prove to myself that I could do it. Boot camp turned out to be really hard. I was held back a month. I wasn't in shape, and I smoked at the time. *That* came to a screeching halt. I was determined, though. And here I am."

"When did you meet A.J.?"

"In technical school. That was hard for me, too. He taught me more than any of the instructors did. He has a gift for stuff like that. I used to get yelled at a lot, and one of the instructors referred to me as the village idiot. I think that offended A.J. more than it did me. From then on he explained things to me in ways that I could grasp."

"Did that make the instructors angry? It was their job to teach, after all."

"A.J. helped me privately after class, in the barracks. We all bunked together. Mason and he are pretty tight, too. We all became buds. First time in my life I felt like I had a family."

I couldn't help myself. I went to Wendall and embraced him. He'd had such a sad childhood. It was amazing that he'd turned out so well. He welcomed the hug, and I felt a tear drop onto my shoulder. I never said a word about it.

"Hey! You're starting our adventurous week without me!" A.J. said in a teasing voice as he entered the kitchen.

"We haven't started eating yet." I released Wendall and hugged A.J. "Where's Marcie?" I asked. "She needs to be outside."

"She's under my covers," A.J. said with a grin. "I peeked in on Dad. He's stacking Z's. I couldn't budge him."

"He sleeps about fifteen hours a day. He'll get up in an hour or two. I'm sure you boys–"

"*Men,* Mama! We are *men*!" A.J. thumped his chest like Tarzan.

I chuckled. "You *men* can find something to do for a couple hours, can't you?"

"I have to wait to call Angela, anyway. It's way too early for the rest of the world. I want to take Dunning four-wheeling to the pond and maybe fish a little."

Wendall's eyes lit up. "Sounds like a plan."

"Me, too," Darin said from the other room. "Me and Marcie want to go fishing."

We all looked up. Darin was holding Marcie in his arms. She was too big to be carried and the sight made us all laugh.

"Marcie missed me last night, " Darin declared. "She's used to sleeping with me now."

"You mean *you* missed Marcie last night, don't you, little brother?" A.J. teased.

"Let's eat," I said. "A.J., grab some plates. Darin, you get the silverware. And, Wendall, you can get the orange juice out of the fridge. I've done my part already."

I knew the bacon would disappear quickly, but I was amazed at how many waffles those boys put away.

By the time Randy got up, my Marines and Darin and Marcie had gone out. I had cleaned the kitchen, washed some laundry for the boys, and taken the frozen lasagna out of the freezer. Even though I'd made it two weeks earlier, I knew it would still be a hit, crammed with Velveeta cheese–A.J.'s favorite.

"I wanted sausage and eggs," Randy said in a disappointed tone as he stared at the waffles and bacon I had saved for him. He had a very hard time dealing with change of any kind–all part of his major depression.

"Please, honey," I said. "It's just for today. This is what we all had. And this is breakfast food, too, right?"

Reluctantly, Randy ate the meal. "Where's A.J.?" he asked.

"Gone fishin'. I hope he doesn't bring any home. We're having lasagna tonight," I said.

"A.J. knows the rules. You catch 'em, ooh and ah, then throw 'em back. They're pets," Randy said.

I laughed. We did consider the fish in our pond pets for the most part.

"Maybe I can get A.J. to change the air filter on the four-wheeler. I have the new one here. Then he can help move all that firewood. Perhaps he'll feel like mowing the lawn, too. It would be nice to have some help around here."

"He's on vacation," Randy said.

"So?"

"Get Darin to help. He's old enough to be responsible."

"Darin isn't a mechanic, and he's not very ambitious when it comes to manual labor."

Randy was silent. He didn't like to talk much anymore. His speech came out in a monotone, and it seemed difficult for him to speak more than a few words at a time. I watched as he rolled his wheelchair backward, heading for the bathroom, where he would "secretly" enjoy a couple of Winstons.

I looked outside to see if I could spot the boys. It was a half-mile to the pond, but the red four-wheeler and Marcie's white fur were easy to spot against the green grass. Our other dog, Otis–a stray we'd acquired only in the past year–played alongside her.

I took a deep breath. I wanted to be on vacation, too. I was tired of mowing, chopping, cleaning, cooking, and everything else that went with having a home and family. Randy had always done the outdoor work, but all of it had been added to my list of chores. Randy was right–I should enlist Darin more often to help with some of it. But I didn't want him to take time away from his schoolwork, and he did, after all, help with a lot of the indoor chores. Which meant I was stuck doing a lot of stuff that wore me out and that was anything but fun.

Maybe, I thought, I could go fishing with Darin and Wendall for an hour or so when A.J. took off to see Angela.

But then, someone had to stay home to watch Randy. He needed twenty-four-hour supervision. Once Darin and I had left him alone to attend a school event, and we'd came home to find him on the floor. And I'd come in from mowing one time and discovered him having a seizure while sitting on the commode.

If only...if only...if only, I thought. Why did this have to happen? Randy and I were supposed to be in the prime of our lives. Our children were almost grown, and this should be *our* time together. Our future, however, looked awfully dim.

I shook my head, refusing to let those thoughts even enter my head this week. I wanted to have fun with my kids and relish the fact that A.J. was home safe and sound.

I heard the four-wheeler pull up and I ran to the door. Uh-oh! A.J. and Wendall just had to show off. They'd brought home their prize catches for everyone to marvel at.

"Don't be mad, Mom. These are just stupid catfish. You've said yourself we have too many of them. But check it out! I think mine weighs about five pounds!" A.J. bragged. "We caught them with pieces of leftover waffles."

Wendall laughed. "I'd like to have mine stuffed and mounted. It's the first catfish I ever caught."

"I didn't fish," Darin said. "Marcie and I scooped up tadpoles. Can I feed them to the chickens, Mama?"

I shook my head and grinned. "I'm sure they'd like that. Hey! Let me take a picture!" I exclaimed. I had just added a new roll of film to my camera. "I'll be right back."

Just then Randy wheeled himself back into the

kitchen, and A.J. hurried to give him a big bear hug. I tried to remember every exchange for my shoebox.

"So this is the famous Mr. Allen," Wendall said as he extended his hand to Randy.

Randy smiled and greeted Wendall. I took more pictures.

After a while A.J. called Angela, then borrowed the car to go to her house, informing me that they would both be back in time for supper. No way would he miss my lasagna, he vowed.

The afternoon was busy, with Darin teaching Wendall how to do flips on our trampoline. Darin was big yet incredibly agile. He could do double back flips like a pro. With Randy in his wheelchair next to me, I sat on the bench outside and watched happily.

"Man! I love seeing how high I can go," Wendall exclaimed.

"How adventurous do you feel today, Wendall?" I called. "I thought we could go horseback riding when it cools off this evening."

Wendall looked at me with troubled eyes. "I don't know..."

I laughed. "Don't worry! I'll teach you how. It's really a lot of fun. You'll be trotting and galloping by the time you leave."

"I may never want to leave," Wendall said. "This is paradise."

"Ha!" I gave a short, harsh laugh, and without thinking, I said, "Maybe it would be if we didn't have so many bills and if Randy hadn't had a stroke and if I weren't worried A.J. might have to go back to Iraq and if–"

"Mom!" Wendall cut me off. "Did God promise us a perfect world? No. Everyone has a cross to bear, right? Everyone feels dissatisfied and unhappy, at least occasionally. We always want more than we've got. There's never enough money, never enough time, never enough anything. Maybe you need to remind yourself more often of the things you're grateful for."

Deeply ashamed of myself, I nodded. "You're right." What else could I say? God had just spoken to me through a nineteen-year-old. I needed to look at my glass as half full, not half empty.

The day flew by. When Angela and A.J. walked in the door, I was pleasantly surprised to see how much difference six months had made. Her hair was longer, and she seemed to have grown another inch or so. At nineteen, she looked like a model, tall and curvy and doubtless the envy of most of her friends.

"You look beautiful," I told her, making her blush.

She was terribly shy and rarely started any conversation, but that was one of the qualities A.J. liked best about her. He said that opposites attract. He was the social guy, and she was the introvert, but they complemented each other like apple pie and ice cream.

Three days passed, and those days were filled with food, fun, and laughter. That had been my prayer, and it had been answered.

Wendall was getting confident on both the trampoline and on horseback. He spent a lot of time with Darin, Randy, and me while A.J. was off with Angela. He was happy to help with any chore, and I soon realized that Wendall was able and willing to tell me a lot more about what was happening in Iraq than A.J.

I encouraged him to do so when we took what soon became our nightly walks. On the fourth evening of the week, as we were strolling around the pond, I said to Wendall, "A.J. told me the Marines find your biggest fear and then cure you of it. Not with therapy sessions but with their own unique style and tactics. I heard about Mason and his fear of heights."

Wendall chuckled. "Getting thrown off that tower was pretty intense for him."

"Do you have any fears, Wendall?"

"I used to. Not anymore."

"What was your biggest fear?"

"Dying."

"And the Marines cured you of it? In the middle of a war?"

"They didn't cure me."

"But you said dying *used* to be your biggest fear."

"Right. But A.J. gets the credit for curing me of it."

"Really?" I glanced at him, more interested than ever. "How?"

"At first," Wendall began, "Mason and I weren't really buying all the stuff A.J. was handing us about God and Jesus. We grew up without Him, so He didn't have an impact on our lives like He did on A.J.'s. When word came that we were going to Kuwait and possibly Iraq, I was scared. *Real* scared. I was afraid of dying. I didn't believe there was anything after this life, and I thought nineteen was too young to pass on."

I agreed wholeheartedly but remained silent so Wendall would keep talking.

"So we get over to Kuwait and do our bridge building

and have time to spare. We start talking about our families and where we lived and...well, you know this already. We got to really know one another, what made each other tick. I listened to Mason argue with A.J. over the whole Jesus story. I didn't want anyone to know my feelings on it. It wasn't any of their business. But I could sense that A.J. knew I was curious.

"And so I kept listening. It wasn't an overnight thing, obviously. A.J. worked hard on Mason. I think he knew he was working on me, too. I started wondering about my way of thinking. I mean, what if there really was a God who sent His son, Jesus, to die on the cross for our sins? What if I believed it and died and it wasn't true? Would I lose anything? No.

"But, on the other hand, what if I *didn't* believe, and it *was* true, and then I died? Would I lose anything? Yes. I'd lose my eternity with Jesus. I thought, Wendall, you haven't got anything to lose by believing, but you've got *everything* to lose if you don't.

"They say there are no unbelievers in foxholes, and it's probably true. I believe in God now because of A.J. Allen. He saved my soul."

I was stunned. "A.J. never told me any of this," I said.

"Because we never told A.J. He doesn't know. He thinks he just told us why he believed. But his story got us to believe, too. What a concept, huh? Mason was the first soul he saved. I saw the change in him. I think he even got over his fear of heights when he started believing in Jesus. But A.J. hates special recognition–he wants to be treated just like everybody else. He doesn't like to take the credit for anything. He works hard, saves lives, and remains humble. You and Randy did something right with him. I see it in Darin, too."

"Thank you," I said. "We certainly tried to be good parents." Pausing for a moment, I asked, "When was your turning point? What did A.J. say that finally made sense to you? Maybe I could say it to some unbelievers, too. I'd love to save someone's soul. They're worth a lot, you know."

Wendall's brow drew together in a thoughtful frown. "I'm not sure you can say what A.J. said, with the conviction he said it with, unless you'd actually met God."

I knew what he must be talking about, but it surprised me to hear that A.J. had told anyone about his near-death experience. He never talked about it. At least, he never had before. I listened as Wendall continued.

"After about a month of listening to A.J. spout off about God loving everybody and all that stuff, I asked him how he could possibly know God was real. Like, what kind of proof did he have? And he said to me, 'I know God is real because I've met Him twice. No one can take that away from me, and I refuse to believe it was a dream or anything else. He personally spoke with me. I would die before I would ever deny Him.'"

"And you believed him," I concluded.

"Yeah," Wendall replied. "It was impossible not to. "He said it with such...*conviction*. I knew he had to be telling the truth. I felt as if God Himself had slapped me in the face and brought me to my senses. How could I not believe? It totally changed me. I wasn't afraid to die anymore."

"Wow." I shook my head slowly. "I guess you were right–Randy and I must have done okay with A.J. I think

I need to put this one in my shoebox."

"The shoebox," Wendall exclaimed. "I hear about that all the time. What a neat idea. And listen" –he gave me a swift grin– "you can be sure you raised your kids right. If A.J. heard your stories and watched how you lived, then so did his brothers. That's why you're so blessed."

"I feel blessed that God brought you into my life, Wendall." I gave him a quick one-armed hug as we walked. "So you were afraid of dying. Mason was afraid of heights. Is A.J. afraid of anything?"

"I think you already know. He's afraid he'll have to kill again. It really upset him. Some people handle things differently. A.J. hated the thought that he'd taken another person's life. Maybe if the kid was older than fifteen or sixteen, or if he'd been holding a machine gun and was about to open fire on a bunch of us...maybe then he wouldn't have felt so guilty. I think the fact that the kid's friend was there and wept so hard for him...well, I can understand why A.J. doesn't want to go through it again."

I nodded. "He didn't have to kill again. Now he probably won't, because he's home. Right?"

"Right." Wendall kicked at a stone on the ground as he walked. His hands were dug deep into his pockets, and the frown flickering across his brow seemed to indicate that he was deliberating about something.

"Is there more you wanted to say?" I asked.

"Well...yeah." Shrugging a little, he said, "We had some really rough stuff happen over the next few weeks, after we were attacked. During the peak of all this, the grunts went in ahead of us. They were trained for the actual fighting. We went after them and had to dispose of the dead Iraqi bodies. It was intense. A.J. puked every time. They all seemed so young."

"*Dispose?* You buried them all?"

"Not individually. We had to put a bunch together."

I shuddered. "Poor A.J. I'm surprised he doesn't wake up screaming in the night."

"He did a few times," Wendall said. "He hated that a lot of them had no I.D. They fought for their country, after all. Shouldn't they get recognition from their own people for dying for their cause?"

I hated talking about politics. I decided to stick with the nightmares. "How long did he have those nightmares?"

"A while. Then one night it stopped. We all asked about it, because nothing we'd say or done had seemed to calm him."

"He just stopped?"

"Yep. He said Jesus came to him in a dream. He wouldn't share the dream, but it had to have been pretty profound."

"Mercy! What a heavy cross you soldiers have to bear." And they'd have to carry them the rest of their lives, I thought, though I didn't say it to Wendall. He'd find out soon enough for himself.

"Hey!" His expression lightening, he said, "May I ask you something?"

"Sure," I said.

"It's personal. Just curious. Do you ever sin?"

I burst out laughing. "Is a frog's butt green?"

Wendall stopped. "No, really. It seems like you don't. You don't cuss or–"

"I drink beer and wine."

127

"That's not sinning. Even Jesus partied–says so in the Bible. He went to all those banquets. What do people think? 'Hey, Jesus, want some wine? No, thanks. I'll just have water with a lemon in it.' Of course He drank wine!"

Wendall was excellent therapy for me. When I'd stopped laughing enough to speak, I said, "Well, I'm a Lutheran, anyway. We're allowed to drink–in moderation, of course."

Wendall raised one eyebrow. "You never answered my question. When was the last time you sinned?"

"Probably about five minutes ago," I answered seriously. "Hey! Look at the lightning bugs! They're everywhere. Aren't they beautiful?"

"They're neat. But you're avoiding my question."

"Yes, Wendall," I sighed. "I sin all the time. I think negative thoughts, and I believe that's a sin. I'm human. I can't help it. It's in our nature. The key is to strive to be like Jesus. But He's a tough act to follow."

"I'm tormented by Satan," Wendall said.

"We all are. He knows our buttons, and he pushes them all the time."

"How do you get through it?"

"I pray. 'Pray without ceasing,' the Bible says. Pray no matter what. Sometimes it's hard to know what words to pray. The prayer the Lord taught us is always appropriate, though. After all, He already knows what's in our hearts."

Wendall nodded, and slowly, softly we recited the Lord's Prayer together.

Our Father, Who art in Heaven, hallowed be Thy name. Thy kingdom come, Thy will be done, on Earth as it is in Heaven. Give us this day our daily bread. And forgive us our trespasses, as we forgive those who trespass against us. And lead us not into temptation, but deliver us from evil. For thine is the kingdom, the power and the glory. Forever and ever. Amen.

My Son is a Marine

EIGHT

"Mom, where's all the chickens?" A.J. asked. "You used to have a lot of 'em."

"I have one rooster and eight hens. That's enough."

"You used to have fifty," he exclaimed as he walked with me to feed them.

"Well, you know–coyotes, opossums, snakes...now I have one rooster and eight hens."

"Don't you wish you had more roosters?"

"No, you only need one. Roosters are like bulls. One bull can service thirty cows."

A.J. began laughing.

"What's so funny?" I asked.

"Harrison surely did miss his calling! He should have been a bull or a rooster. They have harems!"

I laughed. "We can name our rooster Harrison then."

"How has just one rooster survived so many hens?"

"Well, we had three at one point. I gave two away. They just fought all the time."

"Oh," he said.

"Where's Wendall this morning? Are you waiting on breakfast?" I asked.

"Yeah. For a while. He has a stomachache. He says give him an hour and it'll pass."

"I could give him some Pepto-Bismol," I said.

A.J. shook his head. "Nah. This happens to him sometimes. I think he did something to it during the truck wreck and attack. Maybe he squashed something

131

important, and it's repairing itself. Our bodies do that, you know."

"Yes, I know. Does he want to see a doctor?" I asked.

"Nah. He did just before we came here. They can't find anything wrong. They think it's in his head."

"Well, what are your plans today? You only have two more days of freedom, and then it's back to work! Anything fun on the agenda?" I asked.

A.J. smiled. "This week sure went by fast. Why is that, Mom? Why does time always seem to go fast when things are good?"

"Seems like yesterday I was twenty. Today, I'm fort– Well, old enough to not want to think about it. I guess we just have to keep remembering that this old Earth is a staging area. Our bodies weren't made to last forever here. We'll last forever in Heaven."

"You don't look like you're in your forties, Mom. In fact, you're in great shape for being so old," A.J. said, thinking his comment was a compliment.

"Thanks. That's nice to know," I said, rolling my eyes. "So what are your plans?"

"Well, is that jet ski still on the mend?" he asked.

"Are you wanting to take it out?"

"We thought it'd be fun. It's been so hot. What's the deal with it?" A.J. asked.

"I think it's something minor, but I can't figure it out. This is a 'guy' thing, remember? Why don't you and Wendall tinker with it?'

"Great! Do you think Dad can supervise? At least he can give his general opinion, right?"

"If you can get him off the computer. He lives on

that thing."

"So, I've noticed. I guess it's true what they say: Give a person a fish, and you feed him for a day; teach that person how to use the Internet, and he won't bother you for weeks," A.J. said with a straight face.

I laughed.

"Mom..."

The sudden note of seriousness in A.J.'s voice caught my attention.

"Can we talk about something kinda foreign for a minute?" he asked.

"Foreign?" My curiosity was piqued.

"Something we've never talked about before."

"Sure. What is it?"

"I want to ask you about love."

"What kind of love?" I asked.

"True love. Between a man and a woman."

I admit, I swallowed hard before asking, "What do you want to know?"

"How do you know when it's true?"

Caught off guard, it took me a second or two to gather my wits. I had a feeling I knew where this conversation was leading, and I wanted to make sure I didn't step on any land mines in the process. "I can't really give you a definite answer, A.J.," I said. "It's different for everyone."

"How was it for you?" he asked. "Did you know immediately?"

"As a matter of fact, yes. When I met your dad, it was love at first sight. He was so handsome."

"Like Elvis Presley? I know you had a thing for the King. You have all his stupid singing movies."

I had to laugh. "Who wouldn't have a thing for Elvis? He was truly the king of rock and roll!" I winked at A.J., who rolled his eyes.

"Tell me a story, Mom. Tell me the story about you and dad."

I looked into his beautiful brown eyes and smiled. Obviously, he was thinking about Angela. He was nineteen and old enough to want to find true love.

"I met your dad in the Air Force. I was stationed in Okinawa, and so was he."

"I already know all that. Get to the good stuff."

I rubbed his short hair. "The good stuff, huh? Okay. Our first date was great fun. We even kissed. After the third date, I realized I didn't want to go out with anyone else. Just Randy Allen. In 1977, there were a hundred men to every woman in the service stationed in Okinawa. Coming from a high school where I'd never had a single date, I thought I was in Heaven. Giving up all those potential dates for your dad showed me that I was in love."

"So you never went out with anyone else? You got married and had us kids, and all these years you still feel the same?"

"Whoa! That's a lot of questions all at once. Yes, I dated other people. Your dad was a short-timer and left a few months after we'd met. I was on my second tour and had another two years to go. We decided that we would go out with other people. If our love was really true, then it would still be there after we were out of the service.

"So when I got out, I started college, then decided it was time to look him up. We got together, eloped, had you kids, and I think you know the rest of the story."

A.J. shook his head. "I want to hear the good stuff. Tell me about the love part."

"What *exactly* do you want to know?"

"It's been a lot of years since you've dated anyone else. Have you ever thought you missed out because you married so early in life? Have you ever regretted it at all?"

I had to think. "I fantasize about how my life could have been different sometimes. I think that's human nature. I especially fantasize about it these days. Because unless your dad gets better, this is as good as it gets for me, and it looks as if all the fun is over. I admit, sometimes that gets me down. But I've never thought I missed out on something better. Randy has been a great husband and an excellent dad. So, no, I don't regret marrying your dad. I just wish the fun was back. Is that what you wanted to know?"

"Kinda. I'm scared to make a commitment with Angela because...well, what if she finds someone she wants more than me? That would break my heart, Mom."

"How serious is this relationship, A.J.? I know you care about her..."

"I love her, Mom. But is that enough for the rest of our lives?"

I sighed. "I guess I still think of you as my little boy. I can't help it. I'm sorry, honey. But I had no idea that you two were that serious. I thought it was 'high school going steady' stuff. How do you feel when you're with her?"

"Remember that 'love at first sight' you said happened to you? Well, I sorta have the same thing. Except it's more like every day with her is like the first day. When

I'm with her, I'm excited and happy and want each moment to last forever. Is that love?"

I hesitated for a moment, then nodded. "Sounds like it to me."

"Next question. How would you feel if I asked her to marry me?"

"What?" My gaze shot to his. "A.J., you're only nineteen! What about the Marine Corps? You have almost three years left. Would Angela even be allowed to go with you wherever you're stationed?" I hoped I could talk him into waiting until his military duty was completed, but I should have known better.

"Mom!" A.J. exclaimed. "I'm not too young. I know what I want. I want Angela. I think she feels the same about me. Why do I have to wait? I get paid extra if I'm married, so we can live off base. I've thought a lot about this."

Carefully, I suggested, "Do you think possibly it's because you were so lonely in Iraq? You need to give marriage some real heavy-duty thought, honey. It's a huge commitment. I love that girl dearly–don't get me wrong. But you two are still teenagers."

He made a disgusted sound. "Why does everyone make such a big deal out of that? What about the stuff you wrote in that article that got put in the paper? You said something like 'He's not old enough to buy beer, but he's old enough to die for his country.' Same concept. If I'm old enough to die for my country, then I'm old enough to marry the woman I love."

Leave it to A.J. to use my own words against me. I could think of no reasonable argument.

"Would you be mad at me, Mom? If I married

Angela, I mean."

"Of course, I wouldn't be mad at you." I reached over and hugged him. "And you're right. You are a man now. If you want to get married, then you'll do it. I'll stand behind you in whatever you decide. But are we talking about a wedding in the immediate future? Is that what you're thinking?"

A.J. gaped at me for a second, then laughed. "I think the first thing I have to do is ask her if she'd even consider marrying me. If she says yes, we'll go from there. Okay?"

I smiled. "Okay."

"Hey, Mom! Wendall and I have a quiz for you. It's kinda cool. Sarge gave it to us just before we left to come home. We thought it would be fun for you to take it," A.J. said that evening. "Darin did great with it, just so you know there's competition."

I didn't want to take a quiz. "How come you boys aren't tired after jet-skiing all day? You're sunburned, you've been playing hard, and now you want me to take a quiz? Let's eat watermelon instead."

"Ah, come on, Mom," Wendall teased. "It's easy. I promise you won't fail. It's called the Charles Schultz Philosophy Quiz. Are you ready?"

Reluctantly, I agreed. I was handed a pencil and a sheet of paper with six statements:

1. Name the five *wealthiest people* in the world.
2. Name the last five *Heisman trophy winners*.
3. Name the last five *Miss America winners*.
4. Name ten people who are *Nobel or Pulitzer Prize winners*.

5. Name the last half dozen *Academy Award winners* for best actor and actress.

6. Name the last decade's worth of *World Series winners*.

I stared at the quiz for at least one whole minute. "You've got to be kidding. I won't be able to do this," I said, and I handed the paper back to Wendall.

"Don't worry, Mom," Darin said to console me. "I didn't get any of them either."

"What's up with this?" I asked.

A.J. couldn't wait to explain. "The point is that none of us remember this stuff. It might have been big news yesterday, but not today. Achievements are quickly forgotten. Trophies and certificates are put away. Now, try this one."

A.J. handed another sheet of paper to me. I read the quiz and couldn't help but grin from ear to ear. Here are the six statements on this one:

1. List a few *teachers* who aided your journey through school.

2. Name three *friends* who have helped you through a difficult time.

3. Name five people who have *taught you* something worthwhile.

4. Name five people who have *made you feel appreciated and special.*

5. Name five people with whom you *enjoy* spending time.

6. Name five *heroes* whose stories have inspired you.

"I got 100% on that one," Darin said. "I didn't even have to think very hard. They're easy to remember."

"See, Mom? The lesson here is about the people who make a difference in your life. They're the ones that matter. I have your name listed on each one," A.J. said, and then he put his arm around me.

"Me, too," said Darin.

I couldn't say a word. I was too busy crying.

Going to church on Sunday with A.J. and Wendall on my arms made me the happiest woman in the world. We even cajoled Randy into coming with us, despite the car ride being hard for him.

Sitting in the front pew next to those two boys in uniform, I swear, every button I had on popped. What an incredible feeling. I was blessed indeed. The Lord is *soooo* good to me!

Wendall loved the church message on the billboard outside. It read:

How will you spend eternity–in smoking or non-smoking?

We all listened to the pastor's sermon, but none of us could remember much about it. We were too focused on his opening joke, and we talked about it on the way home. It was classic:

A new pastor was visiting the homes of his congregation. It was obvious, at one house, that someone was home, but no one would answer the door. There was noise inside, the lights were on, and the door was ajar. The pastor took out his card and scribbled a Bible verse on it: Revelation 3:20. He dropped it through the door and left.

The following Sunday, he found his card had been returned in the offering plate. It had an added scripture on the back: Genesis 3:10.

He had to see what this was all about and took out his Bible. He burst out laughing when he read the verse.

His original verse said, *Behold, I stand at the door and knock.*

Genesis 3:10 reads: *I heard your voice in the garden, and I was afraid, for I was naked.*

We had one more day left together. I tried not to be sad, but I was. A.J. would get to come home for Christmas, and that was something to look forward to. But it seemed awfully far away. We discussed Christmas and the kind of holiday that it would be.

I looked at Wendall, who was listening quietly. "Hey, Lance Corporal Dunning," I shouted. "I hope you know I expect you here, too! You're family now. You'd better not make any other plans."

I had never seen more gratitude in anyone's face as I did in that boy's right then. He didn't say a word, but he nodded and tried not to blink and let his tears fall.

A.J. wanted everyone's attention to show us a new trick he'd taught Marcie. He had collected all the chewed-up remnants of what used to be her stuffed animals. She still played with the rags. He placed them on the ceiling fans, the pole lamps, and on shelves that were too high for her to reach.

Then he called for her. He said, "Marcie? Where's your baby?"

Immediately she looked up and began to search the ceiling fan and other places where A.J. had strewn her favorite chew toys. It was hysterical.

We had twelve more hours together before we left for Little Rock International Airport. A.J. and Wendall tried to cram another week's worth of fun into those twelve hours.

Deciding to ride the four-wheeler down to the mailbox, I heard a screech, and I cringed. Hadn't A.J. yet realized that he and motorized vehicles did not go well together? It was about half a mile to the mailbox. I looked at the clock and reasoned that five minutes was too long for them to have been gone.

I stepped outside and didn't hear the four-wheeler motor. Something had happened. I knew it with every maternal instinct in my body.

Heart beating fast, I started to run to my car to find them. Then I saw it. They were driving slowly, carrying something white and fluffy on the back. I panicked. I don't have perfect eyes either, but that had to be Marcie. My heart dropped. Not Marcie! Not now! Oh, Lord...please.

My eyes focused in as they got closer, and I let out a sigh of relief. It wasn't Marcie. It was a huge, fluffy white chicken. A dead one.

"What happened?" I asked as they pulled slowly up to the garage.

"It was in the neighbor's yard," A.J. exclaimed. "It just ran out into the road. I couldn't lock up the brakes or we would have wrecked. So I just hit it! It was an accident. Wendall grabbed it, hoping the neighbor wouldn't notice it was missing."

"A.J.," I said, examining the lifeless bird. "Our neighbor knows how many he has."

"So?" A.J. came back, a note of panic in his voice. "Just give him one of our chickens. He'll never know the difference."

I burst out laughing. "That...that *was* one of ours," I managed–barely. "One of our *roosters*." When A.J.'s gaze dropped to the dead bird, his expression baffled, I laughed even harder. "This is one of the roosters I gave away, and, really...A.J., I think the man would know the difference if I replaced his rooster with a hen."

"This will be a good one for the shoebox," Wendall said.

Definitely, I thought, already heading back inside to write it down.

The boys got busy packing, so I decided to mow the lawn. I spent two hours on the riding mower. Then, knowing time was short, I hurried to take a shower before we left for the airport.

After I'd gotten dressed, I walked around the house, looking for everyone. No one was there. The house was completely empty. I began calling out but got no answer. I called for Marcie. Nothing. I looked outside and didn't see Otis either. I panicked.

I put on my tennis shoes and ran outside.

Then I literally fell to my knees at the sight that greeted me. I truly could not believe it. Darin, A.J., and Wendall were walking *with Randy* around the house. They were holding on to him, supporting him, but my husband's feet were actually moving across the ground in shuffling steps. I hadn't seen him walk for months. I didn't even think he was capable of it anymore.

I couldn't take my eyes off the scene before me. It was as if I was in a trance, watching as Randy took step after step, slowly and cautiously, to complete what clearly had been a trip around the house. I thought I'd used up all my tears; it seemed as if I'd cried more tears of joy in that one week than I had tears of pain in the entire last year.

Randy looked steady and confident as his paralyzed foot moved forward and down, forward and down, to complete his steps. A.J. was on his left, the bad side. Wendall was on his right, and Darin was behind him, ready to catch him if he fell backward. No one was speaking. Even Marcie and Otis, walking a few feet away from the men, were watching as if they realized the significance of the event.

What on Earth had happened while I was in the shower?

Whatever it was, I needed to know about it. What had made the difference? What could possibly have such an impact? We'd tried *everything*.

Regardless, I wanted to keep the momentum going. I wanted Randy to gain strength, to get better. To walk again! Then he could send that wheelchair to hell, where it belonged.

I tried to see his expression but couldn't make it out from where I was kneeling. Was he smiling? Was he scared? Was he filled with the Holy Spirit? What was going on in his brain? I couldn't wait to talk to him. I had to know.

Quietly, I rose and went back into the house ahead of Randy and the boys to wait for them–none too patiently, I admit. Finally, they all came inside. I continued to watch in amazed silence as Randy sat back down in his chair. He looked exhausted, but his expression also reflected contentment.

Without a word, he wheeled himself to the bathroom to have a cigarette.

Unable to wait another second, I whispered, "What

was that all about?"

A.J. shrugged. "When Wendall read him that story about guarding the tomb...then what A.J. said...then what Wendall said to Dad. That's when he got up," Darin said.

Bewildered, I looked at A.J., then Wendall, then back to Darin. "What story? I don't know that one. And who said what to whom?"

"Some guy gave it to me at the airport, before we took off for Memphis," said Wendall. "I threw it into my bag. When I was repacking, I came across it. I read it and thought it was really powerful, so I wanted to share it with everyone. You were in the shower. Want me to read it to you?"

With my mouth open slightly, I nodded. "I want to know the whole story. Don't leave anything out. I want to know what happened before I came outside."

Wendall reached down to the coffee table and picked up the two sheets of paper, then began to read. "This takes a very special kind of person, and you will see why. Do you know the story about the soldiers who guard the tomb of the Unknowns? I will tell you. Do you know how many steps the guard takes during his walk across the tomb of the Unknowns and why?

"Twenty-one steps. It alludes to the twenty-one-gun salute, which is the highest honor given to any military personnel.

"Do you know how long the guard hesitates after his about-face to begin his return walk and why he hesitates?

"Twenty-one seconds, for the same reason.

"Why are his gloves wet?

"They are moistened to prevent his losing his grip on his rifle.

"On what shoulder does he carry his rifle? And why?

"He carries the rifle on the shoulder away from the tomb. After his march across the path, he executes an about-face, then moves the rifle to the outside shoulder.

"The guards are changed every thirty minutes, twenty-four hours a day, three hundred sixty-five days a year.

"The guards must have certain traits. To apply for guard duty at the tomb, he must be between five feet ten inches and six feet two inches tall. His waist size cannot exceed thirty inches.

"The other requirements are, he must commit two years of his life to guard the tomb, live in a barracks under the tomb, and he cannot drink any alcohol on or off duty for the rest of his life. He cannot swear in public for the rest of his life and cannot disgrace the uniform or the tomb in any way.

"After two years, the guard is given a wreath pin that is worn on his lapel, signifying he served as guard of the tomb. There are only four hundred presently worn.

"The guard must obey these rules for the rest of his life or give up the wreath pin.

"The shoes are specially made with very thick soles to keep heat and cold from their feet. There are metal heel plates that extend to the top of the shoe in order to make the loud click as they come to a halt. There are to be no wrinkles, folds, or lint on the uniform.

"Guards dress for duty in front of a full-length mirror.

"The first six months of duty, a guard cannot talk to anyone, nor watch television.

"All off-duty time is spent studying the one hundred seventy-five notable people laid to rest in Arlington

National Cemetery. A guard must memorize who they are and where they are interred. Among the notables are President Taft, Joe E. Lewis (the boxer), and Medal of Honor winner Audie Murphy (the most decorated soldier of WWII) of Hollywood fame.

"Every guard spends five hours a day getting his uniform ready for guard duty.

"*Eternal rest grant them, O Lord, and let perpetual light shine upon them.*

"On the ABC evening news, it was reported that, because of the dangers of Hurricane Isabel approaching Washington, DC, the military members assigned the duty of guarding the Tomb of the Unknown Soldier were given permission to suspend the assignment.

"They respectfully declined the offer.

"Soaked to the skin, marching in the pelting rain of a tropical storm, they said that guarding the Tomb was not just an assignment; it was the highest honor that can be afforded to a service person.

"The Tomb has been patrolled continuously seven days a week, twenty-four hours a day since 1930."

Wendall stopped reading and looked up at me. "When I read this to A.J., he said, "Now, that's dedication! Imagine a soldier giving up two years of his life that way. It makes me so proud to hear stuff like that. What if we were killed in Iraq, Dunning? What if we didn't have any identification...like all those young men we picked up? What if that was us? What if we were just buried, and no one ever knew we died for our country? We'd be unknown *there,* in that godforsaken place."

"And then I said, 'God would know,'" Darin added.

Wendall explained that he had seen that Randy was

146

interested in the story and the conversation. He couldn't say why, but he just felt that he'd seen something stirring in my husband's eyes. So he'd taken a chance.

"Say, Randy?" he'd said. "Why don't you be a guard for me and A.J.? If you do, then neither of us will have to die over there, if we ever have to go back. To be a guard, you must walk around the entire house and focus only on your mission. If you do it, then I believe the Lord will protect us both from ever being one of the unknowns in this war. I believe the Lord will honor your request to make sure we're safe. What do you say to that? Are you ready to make the commitment?"

A.J. said that his father hadn't said a word in response to Wendall's challenge, but his eyes had seemed illuminated from within.

Wendall agreed, saying they'd mesmerized him. And then they'd all stood there and watched Randy get out of his chair. He'd stood up straight, holding onto the chairs arms to balance himself. No one had said anything, but together A.J. and Wendall had walked over to Randy's side, and then Randy had put a hand on each of their arms and started slowly walking toward the door leading to the garage.

He'd remained entirely focused, the boys all agreed, taking step after step, as if he truly were trying to be that dedicated soldier who guarded the Tomb of the Unknowns. As if his son's and his son's friend's lives depended on him. Thus determination and willpower had replaced hopelessness and despair. He would do this to save them both. They would never be unknown soldiers.

I heard the explanation, and I'd seen it happening for myself. Still, I couldn't believe it.

And then something flashed through my head. "Did anyone time his walk?"

"I did," Darin said. "From his first step, once he got outside, until he was back at the door was exactly twenty-one minutes."

"My goodness," I said out loud. "There's no such thing as coincidences, right, Wendall?"

The boy winked at me.

NINE

With only a few minutes to spare, I began to rush the boys. Why does it always become a panic situation when you're trying to make a deadline? To add to the panic, Murphy's Law came into play. Anything that can go wrong usually does go wrong.

Randy had a seizure, maybe from exerting himself with the walk. But at least he was in his wheelchair when it happened.

I knew it the moment I heard him wheezing and gasping for air. I ran to the bathroom where he had been smoking and saw him slumped over. He was perspiring heavily. I called for the boys.

Darin rushed to the scene and grabbed Randy. We straightened him in his chair, and I put a cold washcloth in his mouth to insure he wouldn't bite his tongue. I was too late. His mouth was full of blood.

Where are the other boys?" I wailed. "Go get them! We need to get Dad into bed. It takes us a half hour, and we don't have that kind of time."

Darin let go, and I braced myself to take on the extra weight. I looked at Randy and shook my head. Why did this have to happen? Just a few minutes ago, we'd seen him reclaim his courage. He walked again! It was a miracle–or, at the very least, a giant step forward. Those twenty-one minutes had filled my head with positive, hopeful thoughts.

And now this.

In Randy's mind, would this negate what he'd just accomplished? Would he fear he would have a seizure after every attempt to walk?

I heard Darin knock hard on A.J.'s closed bedroom door, and within seconds all three young men stood at the bathroom door.

"Oh, no! Dad," A.J. exclaimed.

Wendall's expression was solemn.

Randy was still in the peak of his seizure. His eyes were rolled back, his mouth was open, blood was dripping from his tongue, and he was gasping for air. Looking at him that way, it would be easy to believe he was dying.

"They always look a lot worse than they are," I said, trying to ease the situation. "The bad thing is that he bit his tongue. If I could just know when these things are going to happen, I could stop him from hurting himself. I know he says he feels dizzy just seconds before they hit."

"Seconds?" Wendall asked. "That's not enough warning."

"Actually, sometimes it is. He felt one about to happen as he was getting out of his wheelchair, and he was able to sit down on the couch before it hit," I said.

"He won't remember this," A.J. told Wendall. "He'll sleep for hours now, as if he ran a marathon."

"It looks rough," Wendall whispered. "Pretty darn rough."

"The worst is about over. I'll need you boys to help me get him into bed. He won't be able to help us at all— he'll be dead weight," I said, glancing at the bed that was located a few steps from the bathroom entrance.

I felt fortunate that the seizure had happened while we were all still home. Darin would have had to call a neighbor otherwise. Plus, what if Randy had hurt himself falling? All those possibilities crossed my mind as I thanked God that timing had been on our side.

"What were you two Marines doing in your bedroom?" I asked. "Darin had to pound pretty hard to get your attention."

Both boys looked at one another and shrugged. It was obvious they'd been up to something...something I wouldn't approve of.

"It's a surprise," A.J. said. "One last thing to put in the shoebox before we leave. It's priceless, Mom. Trust me."

I arched my eyebrows, but then quickly forgot about it with the added chore of getting Randy situated before we left.

I knew Darin would stay home and call me on my cell phone if anything else happened. What a terrible thing to occur just before leaving for the airport. The whole week had been filled with laughter, fun, memories, and a miracle. Why did it have to end like this?

A thought flashed through my mind, and I realized that my subconscious had not been doing its job. *The glass is half full, not half empty.* Shame on me for my pessimism. I wouldn't dwell on it anymore.

I never turn on the radio when I have people in the car. I prefer to visit. As we drove down the lane toward the main road, both boys were looking out the window at the beauty of the farm. Somehow talking would have ruined the moment. I let them both savor the view and dropped my speed to make it last longer.

"I love this place," Wendall said as we turned the

corner. "I'm going to miss it."

"You'll be back for Christmas," I said cheerfully.

"Yeah, but the lightning bugs will be gone."

"Yeah...darn! And the mosquitoes and ticks and snakes, too," I said mournfully.

A.J. laughed. "Winters are neat, too. They're mild, and four-wheeling is still fun. And, we can still ride horses and jump on the tramp. Plus there's all kinds of neat food that Mom only makes during the holidays."

"Like what?" Wendall asked.

"Christmas stuff. We have seafood for Christmas Eve dinner–lobster, shrimp, some noodle dish with crab sauce all over it, a Hawaiian salad thing that's delicious, and these real thick chocolate-coconut brownie things. For some reason we only have those at Christmas," A.J. said sorrowfully.

I smiled as I thought about Christmas. It was still over four months away, but I knew that time would fly by. At least I knew A.J. would be in the States. He'd be safe. Bo would get to come home for the holidays, and it would be joyous. I looked forward to having Wendall meeting Bo. I just knew they would hit it off. Plus, Angela would be spending a lot of time with us, too. I had a feeling she was my future daughter-in-law.

My mind went back to Randy and my thoughts of the glass being half full. Perhaps by then he would be walking with a cane. Perhaps he wouldn't even need his wheelchair anymore.

I tried to visualize what Randy had been like before the stroke. It was hard to remember sometimes. It was hard for me to watch the videos of our trips from years gone by. But Darin and A.J. loved them, and they had showed them to Wendall this past week. Once, I'd glanced up at what they were watching, and saw that it was our trip to Lake Powell. A.J. was just six or seven. Priceless.

Smiling, I'd glanced at Randy, and it was then, seeing his expression, that I realized how painful it was for him to watch his younger, healthy self. As painful as it was for me to watch. We were soul-mates, after all.

Later that night, I'd put all the videos back on the shelf. The boys would probably want to watch them again over the Christmas break. It seemed to be their favorite thing to do–reminisce about the good times. There had, indeed, been so many of them.

"Wait till you see the surprise waiting for you at home, Mom," A.J. said as he nudged Wendall.

Wendall, who'd called shotgun first, was sitting in the front with me. He looked back at A.J. and winked.

My son's tone made my eyebrows go down into a frown. "I don't like that word–*surprise*," I said.

Both boys burst out laughing. I couldn't imagine what it could possibly be, but braced myself for the worst. I really did hate surprises.

"Can you take this roll of film into Wal-Mart and get it developed?" A.J. asked. "We had Marcie on the trampoline doing dog flips. I think there should be some pretty cool pictures in here. Plus, I have some at the pond, some of Wendall riding the horse, one of me holding up the dead chicken, and things you would laugh at. Let's stop at the one that's on the way," A.J. said.

"We don't have time, honey," I said.

"Sure we do! I'll run in and put it in for the hour processing. Then, you can pick it up on your way home,"

A.J. said. "Get two copies, because I'd like them, too, all right?"

I could tell that my son wasn't going to take no for an answer.

"Okay. But, no last minute shopping. I'm having to drive at warp speed as it is," I said, looking at the digital clock in the car.

A.J. was the one who ran in to turn in the film. Wendall and I sat in car with the engine running and the air-conditioner on full blast.

"Will you have the same address as A.J.?" I asked.

"Yeah. We share the same barracks. I have a different room, but it's the same address."

"Would you mind if I wrote you letters, too?" I asked.

For some reason, this really surprised Wendall. He looked at me funny and then smiled. "Well, no. I think that'd be great! I don't get much mail...junk from the Marines is about it."

"You have to write back," I said. "Otherwise it's no fun."

"I will," he promised with a grin. "I'll know my room number when A.J. knows his. Plus I'd like some of those pictures, too."

I smiled, glad that my son had such good taste in friends.

"What are your goals in life, Mom?" Wendall asked as we waited for A.J.

I was taken aback. "Goals? Me?"

"Sure. You have goals, don't you? You seem highly motivated, so I would assume that you still have things in your life you want to accomplish."

"Sure, I–" I stopped, thought for a second or two,

then started again. "Yes, I have lots of goals."

"Name a few."

"Well, Randy–"

"No. Name *your* goals. Not what you wish would happen to Randy. What does Jo Anne wish would happen to her?" Wendall asked softly.

"You know I want a better life. So if Randy could have a better life, then so could I."

"What if Randy can't?"

I was surprised that Wendall would get so personal. "I guess I never thought about that."

"Maybe you should."

"Did you see that plaque a friend of mine made for me on my office wall?" I asked.

"The one about goals?"

"Yes."

"It's my favorite Og Mandino quote. It sums up how I feel about goals. It says 'Never be concerned that your goals are too high. For is it not better to aim your spear at the moon and strike only an eagle than to aim your spear at an eagle and strike only a rock?'"

"I like Og Mandino, too."

"Really?" I was frankly surprised that Wendall had even heard of the motivational author and speaker. "Do you have a favorite quote?"

To my amazement, he did.

"'Beginning today, treat everyone you meet as if they were going to be dead by midnight. Extend to them all the care, kindness, and understanding you can muster, and do it with no thought of any reward. Your life will never be the same again.'"

Before I could respond, A.J. opened the door and

jumped in.

"Let's rock!" he said.

The airport was crowded as I dropped off my two passengers to check-in while I looked for a short-term parking spot. I had to park a good distance away, then jog across the lot to get to the terminal entrance.

It wasn't hard to spot my Marines. They were waiting for me by the automatic doors.

"We have like three minutes," A.J. said.

"Too bad I can't walk you to the gate," I said. "Maybe I could tell the security guard I'm your mom and you two have just come back from Iraq. Think they'd let me slide?"

Wendall chuckled. "Sure! That's a reasonable request. Let's see their reaction, shall we?"

I had to laugh. I would miss these two boys.

"Give me a hug and a kiss! Both of you," I demanded.

They did. Then I watched them take the escalator to the second floor. They waved good-bye before they disappeared.

As I walked back to my car, I let the tears fall that I hadn't cried in front of A.J. and Wendall. They're just a few states away now, I told myself. Not on the other side of the world. But it didn't help. I was going to miss my son *and* his friend very much. I already did.

I had spent so little time at the airport that my parking was free.

"Today is your lucky day," the woman at the tollbooth said. "There's no charge."

I should have felt that way, but I didn't. I wished I

could turn the clock back and start the week all over again.

I stopped in Wal-Mart on my way home and looked at the pictures at the counter before I left. I was so amused at one of Marcie being held by A.J. as Wendall looked on that I had two enlargements made, one each for A.J. and Wendall.

The drive home seemed to take no time at all. I forgot all about the "surprise" awaiting me until I walked in the door. Then I was reminded–forcibly.

There, front and center, was Marcie. She'd been dyed blue.

Those two I'd just put on a plane might be old enough to die for their country and even old enough to get married, but they weren't so old that they'd forgotten how to behave like mischievous little boys.

A month passed. Randy stayed true to his word and had a new lease on life. He was back in physical therapy, his attitude was positive, and he began to work for what he wanted. His biggest desire was to walk again. His second biggest desire was to get his arm, which had been paralyzed from the moment he had the stroke, to work. Chances were slim that it would ever move on its own again, but he remained determined.

I certainly wasn't going to discourage him. We were given exercises to do to stimulate the muscles and trick the brain into thinking it was working. It works like this: If your fingers don't work, you use your other hand and play with those "dead" fingers. You move that lifeless limb up and down, back and forth, and every which way. Your brain thinks it's doing the moving and will start connecting whatever wiring it needs to fix the problem. The brain is the most complicated, incredible, powerful, unexplainable mechanism in the world. You simply need to have faith and believe you have that power. And you will.

A.J. wasn't good at letter-writing, so he would call once a week and fill us in on everything. I was, however, thrilled to get mail from Wendall.

In October, A.J. called and told us that he and Wendall went to their first military wedding ceremony. Sarge and Gurule had gotten married. It was a total shock to everyone. Who would have thought? A.J. laughed and said that Gurule probably carried Sarge over the threshold.

Mason and Logan had cross-trained to be military policemen, so they didn't spend much time with A.J. and Wendall anymore. It was hard to get together with different work schedules and living across the base from one another.

Happenstahl and Harrison had become great friends. Being injured in the same incident had formed a bond between them. Harrison no longer limped from his broken leg, and Happenstahl happily showed everyone his scars. Both were hoping to get purple hearts over the deal.

Wendall was with A.J. on one phone call. He sounded so official:

"Mrs. Allen? I just want to inform you that your two outstanding Marine offspring have an announcement to make from headquarters. LCpl Dunning and LCpl Allen received the highest test scores on their latest training in the combat engineer field."

"Too cool," I said with excitement. "Well done...men!"

Then, in early November, I came home from therapy with Randy to find a message from A.J. on the answering machine.

"Mom! Please pray for Dunning! They just took him to the emergency room with severe abdominal pains. I've never seen him like this! His stomachaches have been getting worse and lasting longer, and he's been missing a lot of work. Then something terrible happened today. I've never seen him in this much pain. Please pray for him! I'll call later as soon as I know something. I wish you were home!"

I waited by the phone for my son's next call. I couldn't imagine anything except an appendix rupture that might have caused acute abdominal pain. As I waited, I looked at a framed reminder of the "Five-Finger Prayer." It's a beautiful reminder of who we should pray for, with the fingers on our hands representing significant people in our lives.

The thumb is nearest you, so you begin by praying for those closest to you. The index finger is the pointing finger. With it, you pray for those who teach and instruct, such as ministers and doctors. The middle finger is the tallest one. It's there to remind us to pray for our leaders because they need God's guidance, too. The ring finger is the weakest finger; it shares a bone. This is to remind us to pray for those who are weak, in trouble, or in pain. The little finger is the smallest and there to remind you to pray for yourself. If you do this prayer correctly, you take care of the needs of the first four groups first, and then your own needs will be put in proper perspective.

The hours dragged as I waited for news about Wendall, trying to reassure myself with the knowledge that, at least, he was in the hospital where, surely, they could fix whatever was wrong with him.

Then the phone rang. It was A.J.

"They found a tumor the size of a grapefruit in Wendall's stomach. They removed it and said it looked bad," A.J. said sadly.

"Oh, mercy." I squeezed my eyes closed. "I thought it was going to turn out to be his appendix."

"Mom, the doctor said Wendall has cancer. The tumor was malignant."

The very word "malignant" made my heart pound even harder. "They know that for a fact?" I asked. "Don't they have to send it off for testing or something?"

"This is the twenty-first century, Mom. They did the tests already. Besides, one of the signs of malignancy, they told me, is if the tumor is black, and it was. The thing is...they don't know if it's spread. He'll need chemo treatments and all that. Mom...I hate this! He's only *nineteen years old!* How can he have *cancer?"*

A question for which I had no ready answer. Despite what one's children believe, a parent can't fix *everything*. Oh, how much I would have loved to be able simply to hit Ctrl+Alt+Delete and make the cancer disappear. But life doesn't work that way. It's one big challenge after another.

Wendall had a fight ahead of him. But he seemed to me to be quite capable of handling anything that life dished out. He had the drive to do whatever it took to succeed. And he would have the Allens at his side for support. More important even than that, he would have

God there, too. Wendall would not let this beat him. He would persevere. And he would win.

I had witnessed the power of the mind, and I knew it could do almost anything. Besides, fighting for one's life is instinctual, part of our nature as humans. We want to live. We want to see another day.

Moreover, what we do on Earth echoes in eternity. A person's character is developed by the tests faced in life. That's how we learn. That's how God works through us. And the task ahead of us is never as great as the Power behind us.

I tried to share some of these thoughts with my son. Wendall would fight. Perhaps he would die. But death would not be the greatest tragedy. Life without a purpose was the greatest waste. The end of physical life wasn't the end of everything.

Then I listened as A.J. talked more about his friend. He kept asking my advice about what he should do, what he should say to Wendall. Again and again he repeated that it was unacceptable–simply impossible–to him that Wendall had cancer. Clearly, I wasn't getting through to him.

Finally, I said, "Who do you go to when you need advice, A.J.? Who is always there for you, no matter the day or the hour? Who have you relied on more than anyone else?"

There was a pause. Then, quietly, calmly, A.J. said, "Thanks, Mom. Think I'll go have a talk with God."

Wendall wouldn't be coming to our house for Christmas. He had several rounds of high-powered chemotherapy treatments to go through, and time was of the essence. He would be spending his holiday in the hospital.

His body had to recuperate from the operation before they started the treatments. He would lose his hair and lose weight, but I could not imagine him losing his spirits. Darin and I wrote him letters almost daily.

He didn't write back. He didn't call. A.J. said he was too weak from all the trauma his body was going through. But we kept writing and sending him our hope and our love.

All the while, I was also watching Randy excel at therapy, and I knew I owed my husband's rejuvenation to Wendall, Darin, and A.J. It was that Tomb of the Unknown story and the support of those three boys that had given Randy the motivation and encouragement he'd needed. He had stood up and walked to save the life of his son and his son's friend.

Did Wendall know what he had done for Randy? Or for me? I made sure I told him in my letters. It was his story, after all.

I told him, too, how much I'd learned about the power of the mind to affect change. A story that had taken less than four minutes to read had forever changed Randy– had, indeed, changed the lives of everyone in our family. I owed a lot to Lance Corporal Wendall Dunning. He had been an incredible friend to my son and to all of us, and we needed him in our lives. I told him that in my letters, too.

I wished I could have told him in person. That not being possible, I was glad A.J. was with him. I was especially glad A.J. was there the day he told me the doctor had given Wendall a bad report that had made him very depressed. The chemo treatments weren't killing the cancer cells. His cancer was spreading. They were going to try a more aggressive drug.

Wendall had confessed to A.J. that he was scared to die.

"He said he was afraid he was going to die right there, in the hospital bed," A.J. said when he called that night. "I asked him, what would you do in this life, right now, if you knew you couldn't fail? He didn't answer me. He just looked at me and cried."

I was swallowing tears myself as I asked, "What did you do?"

"I went and rented *Schindler's List.*"

Bewildered at first, I listened as A.J. explained what on Earth a World War II movie had to do with Wendall's situation. It soon made sense to me. The movie was about a wealthy businessman who lived at the time Hitler was exterminating the Jews. At first, the man didn't care about the Jews. Then something inside of him rebelled when he witnessed how badly they were being treated. He began to have compassion for the Jews, and by the end of the movie he had saved many of them by making them his own workers. He made it appear as if his business was thriving when, in reality, it was plummeting. He didn't care. He wasn't interested in making money anymore. He just wanted to protect the Jews he had grown to love. Still, when the war was over and the Jews were freed, Schindler grieved. He walked outside as the Jews he loved followed. He took the gold Nazi pin from his lapel, held it up, and said, *'I could have bought two more lives with this pin.'* He then looked at his car and began to weep. *'I didn't need this car,' he said. 'I could have sold it and bought ten more lives with the money. I could have done so much more. If only I'd have known. I could have saved so many more lives."*

According to A.J., the movie had had quite an impact on Wendall. When it was over, he'd told A.J. that he had plenty of life left in him and that there were a lot of things he still wanted to do. He didn't have time to die. He didn't want to stand in front of Almighty God and say, *'I could have done so much more.'* No. Not Wendall Dunning.

After that, Wendall changed. He concentrated entirely on getting well. He let A.J. be his encouragement. He allowed himself no more sad days. They might be hard and painful, but they weren't sad. And just as they had done together in Iraq, A.J. and Wendall fought *together* to win the battle against the cancer.

I insisted on talking with Wendall one day when A.J. was visiting him. "I have your Christmas present ready and will be sending it back with A.J. I want you to plan to spend some time with us when you get well enough. You're always in our prayers, but you know that already. We love you, son."

"Thanks, Mom. I just might pop in on you when you least expect it."

Ten

Christmas has always my favorite holiday. Forget all the shopping and presents and parties. It was *family* time! I loved the food and fellowship more than anything else. Anticipating having all three of my boys home together filled my heart with happiness. I could hardly wait to see the look on A.J. and Bo's faces when they witnessed the progress that Randy made. It would, indeed, be a wonderful holiday.

I looked at the beautiful Christmas tree and decided to leave the lights blinking twenty-four hours a day. With one week to go, the bulbs shouldn't burn out. I grabbed a nice-sized box under the tree and smiled.

"This one's for Wendall," I said to myself. "I think he'll get a kick out of it."

Why wouldn't he? I'd packed it full of *fun* things. Some of the items included a bright red Arkansas T-shirt, Billy Bob teeth, some blue hair dye, one batch of peanut butter cookies, a Hot Wheels four-wheeler, a small stuffed horse, a talking bass that hangs on the wall, and a real-looking imitation snake. Everything to remind him of the week he'd spent with us. On the card I wrote: *This box would make an ideal place for memories. I thought it could be YOUR shoebox.*

I spent the last two weeks before Christmas preparing what food I could and freezing it. The decorations were finished. Cards were all mailed. The shopping was complete. Presents wrapped. And therapy sessions were over until after New Year's. You would have thought I was a little kid, I was so excited.

Angela helped with a lot of the baking. We had a ball getting to know one another on a more personal level. I knew A.J. had bought her a ring for Christmas, and I was just dying to see it.

Everyone would start arriving the next day. First Bo, then A.J.

Our tradition was to open one present each on Christmas Eve. I hoped to convince them to open the ones I'd gotten for them. I just knew they'd love them! Here I go, acting like I was five again.

Bo was getting cold, hard cash...all in single-dollar bills. Plus, I wadded them up individually and threw them into a huge box. It would take a good hour to smooth them out, count them, and count them again. I'd made it an odd number to throw him off.

For Darin, I'd bought three sets of monogrammed sweat suits. He kept getting his sweat pants stolen from gym class at school, and I doubted that anyone else would want to wear sweats with DARIN written boldly across the butt. Actually, that part was a gag. I'd just tacked a nametag there to see his expression.

A.J. got a gift for his house–whenever he and Angela married and moved into one. It was a beautiful sequel to his *Footprints* picture, with a frame specially made for it. The anonymous poem read:

Footprints With A Twist

Imagine you and the Lord are walking down the road together. For much of the way, the Lord's footprints go along steadily, consistently, rarely varying the pace. But your footprints are a disorganized stream of zigzags, starts, stops, turnarounds, circles, departures, and returns. For much of the way it seems to go like this but gradually your footprints come more in line with the Lord's, soon paralleling His consistently.

You and Jesus are walking as true friends! This seems perfect but then something happens. Your footprints, those etched in the sand next to Jesus' are now walking precisely in His steps. Inside His larger footprints are your smaller ones. Safely, you and Jesus are becoming one. This goes on for many miles, but gradually you notice another change. The footprints inside the larger footprints seem to grow larger. Eventually they disappear altogether.

There is only one set of footprints. They have become one. This goes on for a long time, but suddenly the second set of footprints is back. This time it seems even worse! Zigzags all over the place! Stops...starts...deep gashes in the sand. A veritable mess of prints.

You are amazed and shocked. Your dream ends. Now you pray:

"Lord, I understand the first scene with zigzags and fits. I was a new Christian. I was just learning. But You walked on through the storm and helped me learn to walk with You."

"That is correct."

"And when the smaller footprints were inside of Yours, I was actually learning to walk in Your steps. I followed You very closely."

"Very good. You have understood everything so far."

"When the smaller footprints grew and filled in Yours, I suppose I was becoming like You in every way."

"Precisely."

"So, Lord? Was there a regression or something? The footprints separated, and this time it was worse than the first."

There is a pause as the Lord answers with a smile in His voice.

"You didn't know? That was when we danced."

I knew A.J. would love his gift, and I hoped Angela would, too. It gave me goose bumps every time I read it.

Randy and I had decided not to exchange gifts. We wanted to spend the money on the kids. I did, however, make him a special card. I thoroughly cleaned and dried the huge wishbone from the Thanksgiving turkey, then painted it gold. On the cover of the homemade card, I drew a cartoon version of Randy and me smooching. Inside, I glued the wishbone, and beneath it, I wrote, *I wish for many more Christmases with you.*

Angela was getting a gift certificate from Wal-Mart. I felt it wasn't personal enough, but A.J. said she would want that more than anything. I would have liked to shop for a girl for a change, but I took his word for it. And, after all, I'd have plenty of other chances.

As usual, Darin was in the traditional Christmas story play at church. He would play Joseph, the husband of Mary. He'd picked that part because he didn't have many lines.

"I just ask for a room at the inn because my wife is about to have a baby," he said. "I don't see myself messing that one-liner up."

I chuckled. "This will be your last year, Darin. We'll all be there for you. You'll be a star."

The one potential fly in my Christmas ointment was that A.J. had told me there were rumblings about sending him back to Iraq. I cringed at the thought. *He did his time! Let someone else go*, I thought uncharitably.

He was confident he wouldn't have to go back. They were training more Marines to be combat engineers and getting new ones assigned to Camp LeJeune all the time. It was only rumblings, he said. Nothing concrete.

Still, I was worried. What if they did send him back there? Could he handle another tour in that country? Was the worst over? The news certainly didn't portray that image. Would he have different responsibilities? Would he complete his four years, then pursue a college degree? Or would he make a career of the Marines?

Worrying about A.J. led me to worry about other things. For instance, what about my other sons? Bo had a definite plan; he was majoring in computer engineering. Darin wanted to go to college in Denver, so he could live with his brother. He was brilliant and had achieved top status at the local high school. We were hoping for a full scholarship. But what if he didn't get it? How would we afford his tuition and fees, much less his room and board?

Would Randy ever be self-sufficient enough for me to return to work? Living off his meager income was becoming more and more impossible. I'd sold everything not bolted down, so I really had no choice. I needed a job.

Would I be able to go back to selling, which was what I knew how to do? I had traveled a lot with sales jobs. Would I be able to leave Randy alone? He had really improved since August. He was walking all over the house, with only the aid of a cane. That was a far cry from being glued into a wheelchair. Still...I looked at his chair in the corner of the room. We weren't entirely free of it yet. And I didn't see how I could be gone for days, leaving Randy entirely alone to fend for himself. I'd be worried sick the entire time.

The future was still foggy, but I knew I definitely needed to earn some serious cash. I decided I would pursue that avenue in January. And in the meantime, I would announce my plans during the holiday and ask for suggestions and feedback, not just from Randy but from the boys, as well.

How nice it was, I thought, that my children were old enough to give me adult advice.

Angela went with me to the airport. She was more excited than I'd ever seen her. We met Bo first, and then the three of us waited an additional two hours for A.J.'s plane to arrive. I winked at Bo when I noticed him watching Angela reapply her lipstick for the sixth time in twenty-minutes.

Bo was excited to be on vacation. We loaded his suitcases into the car and listened to him talk a mile a minute about how crowded the airports were this time of year. It had been almost eight months since I'd seen my first-born. He looked great.

Finally A.J. walked toward us. Angela squealed when she saw him and ran with open arms for a big embrace. It was so sweet to see them together. A.J. looked wonderful. I was expecting someone in a uniform, but he had on civilian clothes.

He smiled at Bo and me, and all I could see was the light in those one-of-a-kind brown eyes.

I couldn't get a word in edgewise on the trip home. I didn't want to. It was a lot more interesting to listen to the conversation the three young people had among themselves. I couldn't remember laughing so much.

The entire week was...well, what can I say? I enjoyed every precious moment. Christmas Eve was wonderful. The meal was delicious, Darin's play was precious, and watching my family open their gifts from me was quite rewarding.

Darin gasped at the sweatpants until he realized the nametag on the butt was a gag. Bo was busy unwrinkling his money and commenting that it would be really cool to find a few wadded-up hundred-dollar bills among the mess of ones. Randy said he would never break the wishbone, so we would be guaranteed years and years of Christmases together. The expression on A.J.'s face when he read his *Footprints With a Twist* was beyond description; I knew he loved it.

I watched as Angela opened up the large box A.J. gave her. I'd helped him do the wrapping, so I videotaped her as she opened up box after box, until the tiniest one was unwrapped. She had to have been expecting the ring, but you wouldn't have known it by her expression. Her face radiated sheer, stunned joy.

I would find out later that she said yes to his proposal of marriage. It was quite a holiday.

A.J. reported that Wendall was having a hard time but that his spirits were high. He was on morphine to handle the pain of the stronger cancer-fighting drug. I hated hearing that he had so much agony in his young life. I hated even worse hearing that his chances of survival were slim. Chemotherapy could control the kind of cancer he had, but it couldn't stop it.

"Could his chances have improved if they'd found it

sooner?" I asked.

"Sure. But they didn't," A.J. replied. "He said they did the tests, and everything always came back normal. They called this a sleeping cancer. Said he's had it for months.   He and I agree it started from our truck overturning in Iraq. He hit the gearshift hard, and maybe that set it off. They say we all have cancer cells. It just takes something to trigger them. Wendall's was probably triggered by that hard blow to his gut. Some of us are more vulnerable than others. It all has to do with our individual body chemistry."

It devastated me to think about Wendall dying. He had so much living left to do. I vowed to pray for him even harder than I had been.

"Mom? Is this the Christmas card you want to give Wendall?" A.J. asked as I helped him pack up Wendall's gifts.

"Yeah. It's supposed to go on top of his box. I wanted you to see it. Isn't it neat?"

"Well...I don't like seeing *Christmas* spelled *Xmas*."

"Read the inside, A.J."

He opened it and began to read the card's legend aloud. "Does *Xmas* take *Christ* out of *Christmas*? The fish, the Greek *ichthys,* is a symbol for Christ that has been used since the days of the early church. In Greek, it is an acronym for Jesus Christ, the Son of God, our Savior.

"Frequently in olden times Christians were forced to worship secretly. The fish symbol served them well at such times because foes of Christianity did not recognize it as a sign Christians used to communicate with one another.

"*X* was the first letter in the Greek word for *Christ*. In the fourth century, copies of the scriptures had to be handwritten, and frequently used terms were abbreviated. The original four gospels were written in Greek, and so the abbreviation of *X* for *Christ* remained.

"The next time you see *X* used in *Christmas* instead of *Christ,* don't think that Christ is being taken out of Christmas. Be reminded that early Christians used the *X* to worship secretly and later to speed up the process of making more copies of the scriptures."

A.J. paused. "I didn't know that."

"I thought Wendall would like this card."

"What's in the box?" A.J. asked.

"You'll see. You'll be there when he opens it, won't you?"

"I wouldn't miss it for the world," A.J. said. "I was just hoping for a sneak preview."

Bo and A.J. had scheduled their flights for about the same time to make taking them to the airport easier on me.

After they departed, I began looking forward to a phone call from A.J. when Wendall opened his gift. When it came, I was rewarded. A.J. said Wendall laughed so hard that he had to hold his stomach. That was *exactly* what I wanted him to do.

Christmas was sure a hard act to follow. But I didn't have time to wallow in post-holiday letdown. I began pursuing a sales job immediately after the first of the year. I put my application in at several places with no luck. I thought I was still very marketable, but employers looked at my age and the fact that I hadn't worked for a while, and those conditions seemed to have a negative influence. It's always easier to get a job if you have a job, I remembered.

I began getting a bit depressed. Just when I needed something to perk me up, I received a phone call from A.J. He was quite excited.

"Mom! I feel like the luckiest guy in the world!" his voice rang out.

"Did you win the lottery?"

"Better than that! Out of, like, two hundred Marines scheduled to go back to Iraq, three of us weren't on the list. And I was one of them. My name isn't on the list! Is that cool or what?"

A.J. was right. This was far better than winning the lottery. My prayers have been answered.

And so a wedding was planned. A.J. and Angela would be married, for now, by a Justice of the Peace in North Carolina. We discussed the details and decided to have a *real* wedding during the summer months. She would move to North Carolina, and they would get an apartment near the base.

I sent Angela to North Carolina with several big boxes of household necessities that I'd been saving for whoever got married first. Included were a set of china, silverware, glasses, can opener, mixer, toaster, linens, and other various must-have items for setting up housekeeping.

They were joined together on January 23, 2004. I couldn't be there in person, but I was there in spirit. I still thought nineteen was too young, but I remembered A.J.'s– and my–earlier comments on the subject. He was old enough to fight on behalf of his country, so he surely was old enough to be married. He was a man, now, a man who knew his own mind. And I'd gotten to know Angela well enough to see that she was mature and fully capable of making a life-long commitment. I prayed for them and wished them every happiness on Earth. And it seemed to me that they were off to an excellent start.

Then something happened that changed everything. On February 6, 2004, A.J. was told he would be leaving for Iraq in twenty-nine hours.

"No way!" I yelled through the phone. "Your name wasn't on the list!"

"I know," A.J. said softly. "But they put it back on. I have to go."

"What's the deal here? Did you tell them you were married? Did you tell them you have a wife now? Maybe they don't know that, and it will make a difference."

"They know it, Mom. It doesn't make any difference."

"Do they simply expect you to pack up and move and take care of all the loose ends in only one day? I mean, business people don't work on weekends. How can you get everything done? What will Angela do by herself? Tell them you need at least a week," I said, as if a mother's words could override a decision made by the major general in charge of Camp LeJeune.

"Mom, I have to go. Believe me, I'm every bit as upset about this as you are, and then some. And Angela hasn't stopped crying since we got the news. Please. I need you to help me out here. I need you to walk her through breaking the lease, calling the phone company and the electric company and shutting off service—things like that—so she can come back home and stay with her parents. Can you do that for me?"

I was so mad at the Marines I could have screamed. I *was* screaming.

It took all the willpower I possessed to calm down and tell A.J. that, of course, I would help Angela get out of there and come back home. But all the while, I was fuming inside. Why were the Marines doing this to my son and his brand-new bride? Surely, he was not indispensable in Iraq. Surely, someone who hadn't already served there could go, while he helped train other combat engineers at Camp LeJeune.

It just wasn't fair! He'd done his time in Iraq. He'd already been there—and he nearly hadn't gotten out alive. Now he had to do a second tour in that horrible place? I wanted to call the president of the United States to protest.

The next twenty-four hours went by in a blur. I couldn't get over my anger. Not even praying was comforting. What astonished me was that A.J. didn't seem anywhere near as angry as I was. He considered himself government property for another two and a half years, and if the Marines wanted him in Iraq, that was where he'd go. It was his duty, plain and simple.

His biggest concern was leaving Angela. His next biggest concern was leaving Wendall.

"Who's going to spend time with him?" he asked me. "Angela and I have been taking him pizza and cheeseburgers and playing card games with him. How will he pass the time while he's getting his treatments? I worry about him, Mom. But I can't think of anything to do about it. I've got to get Angela squared away. We called her brother, and he's coming out to help her move. While she's packing and moving, can you do the phone calling to disconnect things? You still have my Power of Attorney from when I was in Iraq."

"Yes, of course, I'll make the phone calls. Don't worry about Angela. Tell me about Wendall, though. What's his chemo schedule? Doesn't he have his last one pretty soon?"

"He has two more, and then he's supposed to go for three months on a special diet. After that they'll do tests again to see if he's clean. The Marines have already told him he's getting a medical discharge. Of course, he'll get a paycheck for the rest of his life...even if he lives to be a hundred."

Please, God, let him live to be a hundred, I fervently prayed.

A.J. left, as scheduled, and was in Iraq two days later. I spent the next couple of weeks helping Angela tie up loose ends. When she got back to Arkansas, I helped her change her car insurance and get her new license and take care of the other business details of life that one learns as one grows up—and grows older. She was too young to have had to learn all those things yet, but after this, I figured, she'd be a lot more prepared the next time.

In fact, I was amazed at how strong Angela remained through the ordeal. She'd apparently done all the crying she was going to do. She simply put her energy into the tasks to be accomplished and did them. I was proud that she was my daughter-in-law.

She moved in with her sister, but she came to visit me often, which was always a pleasure.

The letters started coming three weeks after A.J. left. He was getting settled in, if there is such a thing in a war or in a place as inhospitable as Iraq appeared to me to be. Even though Saddam had been captured, new training techniques had been implemented, and new requirements had to be met.

After he'd been there for six weeks, I received this letter.

There are a lot of IED (improvised exploding device) strikes here. The insurgents make bombs out of pop cans, rocks...anything. They even make them just by wrapping gunpowder tightly in a dry cloth. We have to be on guard constantly because some Iraqis have attached bombs to guardrails and have blown up entire convoys.

These IED's have to be manually set off, so someone must push a button or whatever is used to ignite them. They use things like car batteries with a long wire or those 'beep-beep' noisemakers that lock and unlock your car.

They watch everything we do. When we get close, they blow up the bombs. It's a total war zone here. So far there have been more injuries than fatalities. The shrapnel flies everywhere when these explosions happen.

We've been taking every precaution and have learned every possible trick in the book. It's the suicide bombers that are the biggest worry. They don't care about their own lives. They're ready to die in order to kill us.

I'll be heading for northern Iraq in two days. I won't get a lot of opportunity to call or write for a while. Northern Iraq's nickname is IED Strike Alley. And I'll be back in the middle of it all.

I guess I can tell you this now. While I was in North

Carolina, I had guard duty twelve hours a day. The hours were from 2000 hours (that's 8:00 p.m. to you) to 0800 hours (8:00 a.m.). Many nights the skies were clear, and I could see nothing but stars forever and ever. I was all alone most nights and couldn't help but look at all those stars just hanging up there. Sometimes I would see a shooting star and make a wish. Have you ever prayed for twelve hours straight, Mom? That's what I did a lot of the time. I prayed I would never have to go back to Iraq. I prayed harder than I ever prayed before. Something gnawed at me, because I sensed God's answer would be no.

And it was. Here I am. So obviously God said "No. You're going back." I don't understand things sometimes, but I know I have to accept them. God has a reason for everything, even if I'll never know what it is. I don't think anyone can figure Him out. All I can say is that I prayed hard, Mama. I begged God. He must have a pretty good reason to send me back here. All I can do is keep doing what I do and hope I fulfill whatever mission I'm supposed to accomplish here. I don't want to fail the Lord. He's been there for me too many times.

I miss everyone all over again. I'm already homesick and lonely and waiting for letters, and I just got here. The weather is warm, not scalding hot yet. We took over the Iraqi base called Anaconda. We are the only Marine unit (Bridge Alpha) on the Army base. There's about a hundred and thirty of us.

Speaking of the Army, are they ever spoiled! They get normal food and sleep in real beds. It must be nice to have a choice of cereal or sandwich and actually have ice in your drinks.

The locals here are just like everyone at home. Ninety to ninety five percent just want to go to work and come home and live their lives. It's that other small percent that makes things bad.

I have to deal with locals every day. You can't walk out among them and think one of them might be wired, or you'll never focus on your job. We're trying to rebuild Iraq, and that will take time. The Marines here are repairing the bridges, guiding traffic, and making sure everything is secure.

The one thing I've noticed more than anything else is how everyone bows their heads and prays before eating, sleeping, and working. It's a good feeling, because we all depend on God, and that's the way it should be.

Mom, I feel as if God has made a fist and stuck me right in the middle of it to protect me. Please don't worry.

You can do something for us over here, though. If anyone asks, tell them not to forget about us. Keep us in your hearts and prayers.

I love you way over the moon!

A.J.

March was almost over. I still hadn't found a job. I applied to be a waitress at one restaurant that promised $200 a night in tips due to their license to serve alcohol. I had a great interview with a young man who seemed to really like me.

When two weeks passed, I noticed the job was still in the paper, so I called him. He was reluctant to tell me why he didn't want to hire me, but he finally admitted his reason: "You remind me of my mom, and I could never boss her around."

I began to get depressed. Darin would be graduating this year, and he would be moving to Denver with his brother–scholarship or no scholarship. He'd pay for his own college, he said. He just wanted out. Randy still needed a lot of help, and Darin wanted his freedom. I couldn't blame him. He'd spent the last three years largely staying at home. He wanted to have his own life.

It's an amazing thing when you hit bottom. God seems to know when you're about to lose it, because something phenomenal always happens.

Wendall Dunning showed up at our door.

I can't imagine the look of surprise on my face, but it had to have been there, judging by the expression on his.

"Hey, Mom," he said with a smile that was uniquely his.

"How did you ever find your way back here?"

"I pay attention. I have the directions up here," he said, pointing at his crew cut.

I grabbed him and hugged him, then just as quickly push him away, saying, "Let me look at you. You're too skinny, but you look darn good."

"I feel good," he said, his tone confident.

"Where are your bags? You do plan to stay awhile, don't you? A.J.'s room is empty."

He laughed. "I was hoping you'd ask."

He went to his car, got out two suitcases, and came inside.

"I haven't heard from you since A.J. left for Iraq. Fill me in!"

"I drink my coffee black," he hinted.

I smiled. It was just a little after 10 a.m. I still had coffee in the coffee pot. I poured him a cup, and we sat down at the kitchen table.

"I guess you know I got a medical discharge. It's still honorable, but under different circumstances."

"What about future treatments? They'll still pay for everything, right?"

Oh, sure. They've taken care of me. I even financed that car through them. But I'm officially out now and didn't have any place to go, really. I kept thinking about this farm, and, well...the memories are good here."

"I'm glad you feel that way. Can you tell me about your cancer? Are you free of it now?" I asked with considerable trepidation.

Wendall took a sip of coffee, then nodded. "I'm in remission. The chemo was so intense, I begged God to just let me die. I didn't know how much more of it I could take. It was really...well, it was awful."

I reached across the table and patted his arm. "A.J. said you handled it like a real trooper. He was so proud of you. I can't wait to write him and tell him you're here."

"I already wrote and told him I was planning to come. Maybe he'll get a chance to call soon. He's the best friend I ever had, you know."

"He's a wonderful son. I know he'd be a wonderful friend. But so are you, Wendall. You've been a really important person in all our lives. We care about you."

"One of the main reasons I came here was because I wanted to tell you something. I have the time now to travel and the means, to some degree, with my disability from the Marines. But I...well, I'd like to tell you a story."

I had to smile. I gestured to indicate that I was ready to listen.

"A.J. has made a profound impact on my life,"

Wendall said. "He's made one on *a lot* of people's lives. You know about some of them. Mason and the rest of us stuck in that truck wreck in Iraq."

Pausing for a moment, Wendall looked at his coffee mug, frowning thoughtfully. Then, raising his gaze to meet mine once more, he continued. "When this cancer thing hit, I thought at first that I was stronger than it was. But then it just got to me. The days were so long and the pain so intense. I became immune to the morphine. I actually thought God was mad at me for something. A.J. heard all this because we talked about everything under the sun. He told me the cancer wasn't my fault, but that I shouldn't blame God for it, either. I told him my sins were probably so many before I finally believed in God that...well...He was punishing me."

I shook my head sadly. "God doesn't work that way, Wendall."

"I know that now," he replied. "A.J. told me a story that went something like this: The Lord came to see a man named Wendall Dunning. Wendall believed that his sins were so great that the Lord decided He'd have to punish him instead of simply forgiving him. The Lord told this young Marine that he was going to take him to the ocean. And so they flew there together. They were in the middle of all this vast water when they spotted two buoys bobbing aimlessly. The Lord had Wendall sit on one, and He sat on the other. The Lord had a glass of water in His hand, and He gave it to Wendall and said, 'These are all your sins. I've put them in this glass of water.' Wendall said, 'Lord! There are millions of drops that make up that amount of water. There are so many!' Then the Lord asked him to dump the water into the ocean, and so he did. The Lord then said, 'Now, My son. Get back that glass of water and hand it to Me.' Wendall was shocked at such a request and said, 'But, Lord! How can I? It's been mixed up with all this water! It's gone forever! I can't possibly find it in this ocean. And the Lord replied, 'Neither can I.'"

Finishing the story, Wendall held my gaze with a smile.

"That's a great story," I said.

"I put in my shoebox," he said.

"So now you know you're forgiven. See how it all works?"

He shook his head. "That's only the beginning. A.J. told me this story and helped me get rid of my misplaced guilt. The next day, the doctors said they couldn't do anything else for me. The cancer had spread, and the heavy drugs weren't working like they'd hoped. They gave me a matter of weeks to live. When A.J. came to see me that day and I told him, he refused to buy it. And he told me about something that he does on a daily basis. He told me that, at the age of three, he met God, and God told him this secret to staying healthy. He said that God told him that he would be able to share it with others as the need arose–and that it would always be on a one-on-one basis."

My eyes widened. A.J. had never said any of this to me. Then, I realized, I'd never been in need of knowing.

Fascinated, I listened as Wendall continued.

"He told me that I had to lie perfectly still or stand up straight–that it would work either way. Then I was to close my eyes and rid myself of any thoughts other than what I was about to feel. I was to imagine the Lord's finger coming out of the sky and touching the top of my head. I did–I felt it immediately. It was like a jolt but a gentle one. At that moment, my head felt the light...the light from Him. It started traveling down my body, fixing everything as it went."

Wendall gave his head a quick shake. "It's impossible to describe the sensation. God was actually healing me. Not by medicine, not by anything of the Earth, but by Almighty God. The light within me *was* God. So then God was in control of my body that He wanted to be perfect. I had to give myself up entirely to Him, to trust in Him to heal me. To believe He *wanted* me to be healed. That was the hardest of all–to have faith that He had needed me for some important purpose in life.

Drawing a deep breath, Wendall admitted, "That was the hardest part–having faith that He needed me for some important purpose. That there's a *reason* for my life to continue. Once I accepted that, once my faith was strong enough, the light was able to do its work. It traveled downward, stopping in the trouble areas, where the darkness was deepest. I did just what A.J. told me to do. I stayed focused. I traveled with the light. I knew my biggest trouble area–my abdomen. As I expected, the light stayed there a long time before it continued down the rest of my body.

"When it reached the end, it was so strong that it poured out of my fingertips and toes and nostrils and ears. I was totally surrounded by it, and my body was perfect. And the greatest thing about this? While I was in the light, I had no pain. None at all. Sometimes I would stay in the light for a full hour. It's hard to keep up the intense concentration it requires to maintain it for longer than that.

Leaning forward on his elbows, fixing me with his gaze, Wendall said, "The key here is faith. To keep trusting that God is inside me, healing me. The healing wasn't instant. I had to persevere because healing is a *process*, not a single event. So much of my body had been eaten up by cancer, there was a lot of work to do. But as A.J. told me, I had to keep believing with my whole heart and soul that I was getting better each time I did it. And eventually, it was clear to me that he was right. I was doing it each day, and each time was shorter than the last because the light had repaired more of the damage, so it was easier for it to travel through me.

"And then one day I was doing this, and there were no dark areas left. My mind knew it, and so did my heart. We—the light and I—traveled together and saw that my abdomen was free of all darkness.

Leaning back in his chair, Wendall took a sip of his coffee. "I do this at least five times a week now to keep my body free from the cancer. I also do it because I feel so protected and loved in His light.

Grimacing a little, he finished, "That's the best way I can describe it. A.J. explained it to me much better than I just did. He's lived in the light a lot longer than I have."

I was too mesmerized to answer immediately. Slowly, I shook my head. "I think you explained it just fine. I'm...I'm in awe."

"So was I," Wendall said. "And I'm here today to tell you that the doctors couldn't find one cancer cell left in me. I'd been doing this..." He gave a quick laugh. "A.J. calls it a 'light exercise.' I'd been doing it for forty-seven days when they told me the news. I'm only sorry A.J.

wasn't there to hear me shout–and to shout with me."

I heaved a sigh, blinked a couple of times, and tried to gather my wits. "Wendall...I don't know what to say. It's incredible. I'm so happy for you."

"Me, too," he replied. "And I want you to know, I'll be forever grateful to you for having your son. There'd be a big hole in this world if he hadn't been born–or if he'd died way back when." Hesitating briefly, he added, "I also want to tell you that I think I know why A.J. had to go back to Iraq. His name wasn't on the list, remember."

"Boy, do I remember," I replied my anger surging all over again.

"Well, I think God put it back there."

"What?" I exclaimed, incredulous.

Wendall nodded. "A.J. is needed in Iraq. And I truly feel he's protected from any harm. He's one of His, and people know that instantly when they meet him–even if they don't entirely understand what it is about him that's special, if you know what I mean."

"I think so," I murmured. "But–"

"Wait. Let me finish. Meeting A.J. is the most important thing that's ever happened to me. He's saved my life, literally, twice now. And I've watched him save others' lives, too. It's his gift. I believe it's also his job– his purpose, the reason God needs him. And I have faith that God will take care of him so he can go on saving lives."

I didn't have words to express the mix of emotions Wendall's insight had caused inside me. One thing, though, was clear: He was right. A.J. had been living in the light since he was three years old. God had saved him then, and again when he was fourteen, and He'd sent him home safely from the war the first time. If A.J.'s faith was strong enough to lead another person to cure himself of cancer, surely, I could find it in me to have faith that God would protect my son this time, too.

I wanted to talk more with Wendall about his experience with the light–perhaps try it myself. And I certainly wanted him to tell Randy what he had told me. But I'd had as much intensity for one morning as I could handle. I needed to gather my thoughts and bring things back to a more mundane plane of existence.

"What are your plans now?" I asked.

Wendall shrugged a little. "I'd like to stay here for a while, if that's okay. Then I'd like to volunteer or get a job in a hospital–maybe even the Children's Hospital, where I could share with the kids the things that A.J. shared with me. I'd like to make a difference in someone's life, and I think I can now. I have a great story to tell, don't you think?"

"Yes, I definitely think you do," I said.

Wendall unpacked his bags, put his clothes in the empty dresser that A.J. had used, then went out to walk over to the pond. Randy was asleep, and Darin was at school. I decided to write a letter to A.J.

Dear A.J.,

How's my favorite Marine? I have much to tell you.

You already know that Wendall is here. His letter beat mine. He's in remission, and I think he'll stay that way. He looks great, but I plan to feed him my Velveeta lasagna to put some meat back on his bones.

The church had a great slogan on their bulletin last week. Here it is: CH _ _CH What's missing?

Here's my story of the day for you:

A young Marine was newly assigned to a post in a foreign country. His sergeant watched him the first day and knew the going was rough. The Marine's tools broke, his canteen was leaking, and he didn't have enough water. He was asked to drive a truck to pick up parts, and the vehicle overheated in the hot weather. He was having a terrible day.

That evening the sergeant stopped by the Marine's tent just as the young man arrived. The Marine paused briefly at a tree outside the tent and reached toward the tips of the branches with both hands.

Then something happened to the weary young Marine. He underwent an amazing transformation. He smiled at his buddies, introduced them to the sergeant, and began to talk positively about everything but the events of that miserable day.

The young Marine walked the sergeant back to his Jeep and thanked him for stopping by.

The sergeant's curiosity got the better of him. He asked the young man about the significance of the tree.

"Oh, that's my trouble tree," the Marine said. "I know I'll have troubles on the job. It can't be helped. But those troubles don't belong where I live. My buddies and I made a pact that we'd leave our troubles out on that tree, and when we leave for work the next day, we can pick them up again.

The young Marine smiled. "Funny thing is, when I come out of the tent to pick them up, there aren't nearly as many as I remembered hanging up the night before."

When you were four years old, A.J., you told me you knew all the words to the Twenty-third Psalm. I was amazed, because it was long. And so I challenged you. You closed your eyes, folded your little hands, and began to recite: 'The Lord is my shepherd. That's all I want.'

Son, I might have laughed to myself at the time, but, in truth, you were right: the Lord is your shepherd. And that's all you'll ever need. Be so strong that nothing can disturb your peace.

I love you way past all the stars in the universe,
Mom

Crisco's™
"Ultimate Peanut Butter Cookies"
(A.J.'s Favorite)

1 cup Crisco™ Butter Flavored Shortening
1 ½ cups CRUNCHY peanut butter
2 ½ cups brown sugar
6 Tablespoons milk
2 Tablespoons vanilla

Mix above ingredients together until creamy.

Add:
2 eggs
Mix again.
Sift the following three items together:
3 ½ cups flour
1 ½ teaspoon salt
1 ½ teaspoon baking soda

Add above to mixture

Drop by spoonfuls onto an un-greased cookie sheet. Press down with fork.

I use a convection oven at 375 degrees for approx 9 minutes depending on how big you make them. Conventional oven (same temp) takes longer. Keep an eye on them. Don't let them burn.

Here's the biggest secret to this recipe: MAKE SURE YOU USE THE CRISCO™ BUTTER FLAVORED SHORTENING, or it won't turn out soft at all. Very important!

My Son is a Marine

Meet the author:

Jo Anne Allen, the mother of three grown sons, lives on her family's farm in Arkansas.

She started writing during a five-day electrical outage in 2000. As she described it: "With His guidance I spent the Christmas holiday putting pen to paper, literally. I felt overwhelmingly inspired to write a book. Doing the majority of the writing by hand and candlelight, I felt the Lord's hands on my shoulders the entire time. It was as though He wrote it."

She went on to self-publish six short volumes of Young Adult books, and was the recipient of the American Christian Writers "Writer of the Year" Award. Her son's deployment to Iraq and her own personal crisis inspired MY SON IS A MARINE.

Jo Anne now views everyday as another step in a journey filled with love and adventures and knows that the Lord will see her through whatever comes her way.

You can visit Jo Anne at

www.mysonisamarine.com

Launched by readers, writers, and publishers, **Support Our Soldiers (SOS) America, Inc.**, is a non-for-profit 501 (C-3) corporation devoted to helping our troops overseas and in military hospitals. Many of our deployed men and women do not receive mail or treats from home. Many of the recovering soldiers could use a helping hand.

You can lift soldiers' spirits by showing that you appreciate their effort and sacrifice. Notes and pictures from kids mean a lot to our troops–lets them know what they're fighting for.

Tips on writing letters and a list of needed supplies can be found at our website. If you and your family, organization or school would like to correspond with military units, sign up for our newsletter.

Treat a Wounded Soldier to a Trip: SOS America organizes holidays for wounded soldiers and their spouses. Your donations can help sponsor a get-away for a couple. See details at our web site....

SOS America, Inc.
55 Bergen Street, Brooklyn, New York 11201
Tel No: (718) 237-1097 (Ext 10)
www.sosamericainc.com